Building Single-page Web Apps with Meteor

Build real-time apps at lightning speed using the most powerful full-stack JavaScript framework

Fabian Vogelsteller

[PACKT] open source*

PUBLISHING   community experience distilled

BIRMINGHAM - MUMBAI

Building Single-page Web Apps with Meteor

First published: January 2015

Production reference: 1210115

Published by Packt Publishing Ltd.
Livery Place
35 Livery Street
Birmingham B3 2PB, UK.

ISBN 978-1-78398-812-9

www.packtpub.com

Cover image by Tyler Leavitt (tslclick@gmail.com)

Credits

Author
Fabian Vogelsteller

Reviewers
Riccardo Mancinelli
Rohit Mukherjee
Isaac Strack

Commissioning Editor
Pramila Balan

Acquisition Editor
Richard Brookes-Bland

Content Development Editor
Priyanka Shah

Technical Editor
Ankita Thakur

Copy Editor
Vikrant Phadke

Project Coordinator
Neha Thakur

Proofreader
Lawrence A. Herman

Indexer
Hemangini Bari

Production Coordinator
Manu Joseph

Cover Work
Manu Joseph

About the Author

Fabian Vogelsteller became interested in web technologies at the age of 14. He developed a skill set ranging from graphic design to coding PHP to Python, ActionScript, Objective C, HTML, and CSS, and fell in love with JavaScript. He has worked as a freelance web developer for over 14 years and is the creator of the open source feindura Flat File CMS. Fabian is a strong advocate of open source software and has built and contributed to many open source libraries and projects. In recent years, Meteor has become his passion and is his primary tool of choice. He currently works for start-ups in Berlin, extending his skills to web development for larger applications.

Acknowledgments

I would like to thank Marjorie, my partner, for the strength in my life and my beautiful son, Joschua, for being my son.

About the Reviewers

Riccardo Mancinelli acquired a degree in electronic engineering. He has more than 9 years of experience in IT, specializing in frontend and backend software development. He is currently working as an IT architect consultant and senior Java developer. He loves any tool and programming language that will make achievement of his goals easier and faster. Besides programming, his favorite hobby is reading.

Rohit Mukherjee is a final year student of computer engineering at the National University of Singapore (NUS). He has spent some time in Zurich, Switzerland, studying graduate courses in computer science at ETH, Zurich. He has worked in financial and healthcare technologies and enjoys working his way through the stack.

> I would like to thank my parents and Pratish Mondal for their support.

Isaac Strack is an Adobe DPS solutions consultant, and has worked in MIS, web, and app development for over 15 years. An inventor, author, and design technologist, he currently specializes in cutting-edge web technologies, digital publications, and mobile applications. Isaac is the co-captain of the Meteor SLC Meetup group, regularly meeting other meteorites to discuss and share their passions and projects. He is a volunteer for the board of directors of Wasatch Institute of Technology, Utah's first computer science high school (http://wasatchinstitute.net). He is also a member of the Adobe STEAM team, helping promote and foster STEM and Arts education for students of Utah, preparing them for future jobs. As a father of four girls, his passion and energy for technology education are seen through the various presentations, events, and classes he participates in each year. He firmly believes that education is the great equalizer, bringing confidence, prosperity, and joy to everyone, regardless of background or ethnicity.

www.PacktPub.com

Support files, eBooks, discount offers, and more

For support files and downloads related to your book, please visit www.PacktPub.com.

Did you know that Packt offers eBook versions of every book published, with PDF and ePub files available? You can upgrade to the eBook version at www.PacktPub.com and as a print book customer, you are entitled to a discount on the eBook copy. Get in touch with us at service@packtpub.com for more details.

At www.PacktPub.com, you can also read a collection of free technical articles, sign up for a range of free newsletters and receive exclusive discounts and offers on Packt books and eBooks.

https://www2.packtpub.com/books/subscription/packtlib

Do you need instant solutions to your IT questions? PacktLib is Packt's online digital book library. Here, you can search, access, and read Packt's entire library of books.

Why subscribe?
- Fully searchable across every book published by Packt
- Copy and paste, print, and bookmark content
- On demand and accessible via a web browser

Free access for Packt account holders

If you have an account with Packt at www.PacktPub.com, you can use this to access PacktLib today and view 9 entirely free books. Simply use your login credentials for immediate access.

Table of Contents

Preface

Thank you for buying this book. You made a great choice for a new step in frontend and JavaScript technology. The Meteor framework is not just another library that aims to make things easier. It is a complete solution for a web server, client logic, and templates. Additionally, it contains a complete build process, which will make working for the Web by chunks faster. Thanks to Meteor, linking your scripts and styles is a thing of the past, as the automatic build process takes care of everything for you. Surely, this is a big change, but you will soon love it, as it makes extending your app as fast as creating a new file.

Meteor aims to create single-page applications where real time is the default. It takes care of the data synchronization and updating of the DOM. If data changes, your screen will be updated. These two basic concepts make up a lot of the work we do as web developers, and with Meteor this happens without any extra line of code.

In my opinion, Meteor is a complete game changer in modern web development. It introduces the following patterns as defaults:

- Fat clients: All of the logic resides on the client. HTML is only sent on the initial page load
- JavaScript and the same API are used on both the client and the server
- Real time: Data synchronizes automatically to all clients
- A "database everywhere" approach, allowing database queries on the client side
- Publish/subscribe patterns for web server communication as the default

Once you have used all these new concepts, it is hard to go back to the old way of doing things where so much time goes only into preparing the app's structure while linking files or wrapping them into Require.js modules, writing endpoints, and writing code to request and send data back and forth.

While reading this book, you will be introduced step by step to these concepts and how they connect together. We will build a blog, with the backend to edit posts. A blog is a good example, as it uses listings of posts, different routes for each post, and an admin interface to add new posts, providing all we need to fully understand Meteor.

What this book covers

Chapter 1, Getting Started with Meteor, describes the necessary steps to install and run Meteor, while also going into details about the folder structure of a Meteor project and, in particular, the Meteor project we will build.

Chapter 2, Building HTML Templates, shows how reactive templates are built using handlebars such as syntax and how simple it is to display data in them.

Chapter 3, Storing Data and Handling Collections, covers database usage on the server and the client sides.

Chapter 4, Controlling the Data Flow, gives an introduction to Meteor's publication/subscription pattern, which is used to synchronize data between the server and the clients.

Chapter 5, Making Our App Versatile with Routing, teaches us how to set up routes and make our app behave and feel like a real website.

Chapter 6, Keeping States with Sessions, discusses the reactive Session object and how it can be used.

Chapter 7, Users and Permissions, describes the creation of users and how the login process works. At this time, we'll create the backend part for our blog.

Chapter 8, Security with the Allow and Deny Rules, covers how the data flow can be limited to certain users to prevent everybody from making changes to our database.

Chapter 9, Advanced Reactivity, shows how we can build our own custom reactive object that can rerun a function based on a time interval.

Chapter 10, Deploying Our App, covers how to deploy the app using Meteor's own deploy service and also on your own infrastructure.

Chapter 11, Building Our Own Package, describes how to write a package and publicize it on Atmosphere for everybody to use.

Chapter 12, Testing in Meteor, shows how packages can be tested using Meteor's own tinytest package, as well as using third-party tools to test the Meteor application itself.

Appendix, contains a list of Meteor commands as well as iron:router hooks and their descriptions.

What you need for this book

To follow the examples in the chapters, you will need a text editor to write the code. I highly recommend Sublime Text as your IDE, as it has a wide range of plugins for almost every task a web developer could think of.

You will also need a modern browser to see your results. As many examples use the browser console to make changes to the database and to see the results of the code snippets, I recommend Google Chrome. Its Developer tools web inspector has everything a web developer needs to work and debug websites with ease.

Additionally, you can use Git and GitHub to store your success every step along the way and in order to go back to the previous versions of your code.

The code examples for each chapter will also be available on GitHub at `https://github.com/frozeman/book-building-single-page-web-apps-with-meteor`, where each commit in this repository correlates with one chapter of the book, giving you an easy way to see what was added and removed in each step along the way.

Who this book is for

This book is for web developers who want to get into the new paradigm of single-page, real-time applications. You don't need to be a JavaScript professional to follow along, but certainly a good basic understanding will make this book a valuable companion.

If you have heard about Meteor but haven't yet used it, this book is definitely for you. It will teach you everything you need to understand and use Meteor successfully. If you have used Meteor before but want to get a deeper insight, then the final chapter will help you improve your understanding of custom reactive objects and writing packages. Testing is probably the least covered topic in the Meteor community right now, so by reading the final chapter, you will easily gain an understanding of how to make your apps robust using automated tests.

Conventions

In this book, you will find a number of styles of text that distinguish between different kinds of information. Here are some examples of these styles, and explanations of their meanings.

Code words in text, database table names, folder names, filenames, file extensions, pathnames, dummy URLs, user input, and Twitter handles are shown as follows: "With Meteor, we never have to link files with the <script> tags in HTML."

A block of code is set as follows:

```
<head>
  <title>My Meteor Blog</title>
</head>
<body>
  Hello World
</body>
```

When we wish to draw your attention to a particular part of a code block, the relevant lines or items are set in bold:

```
<div class="footer">
  <time datetime="{{formatTime timeCreated "iso"}}">Posted
  {{formatTime timeCreated "fromNow"}} by {{author}}</time>
</div>
```

Any command-line input or output is written as follows:

```
$ cd my/developer/folder
$ meteor create my-meteor-blog
```

New terms and **important words** are shown in bold. Words that you see on the screen, in menus or dialog boxes for example, appear in the text like this: "However, now when we go to our browser, we will still see **Hello World**."

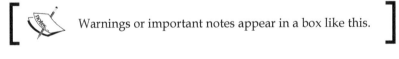

Warnings or important notes appear in a box like this.

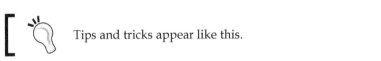

Tips and tricks appear like this.

Reader feedback

Feedback from our readers is always welcome. Let us know what you think about this book—what you liked or may have disliked. Reader feedback is important for us to develop titles that you really get the most out of.

To send us general feedback, simply send an e-mail to feedback@packtpub.com, and mention the book title through the subject of your message.

If there is a book that you need and would like to see us publish, please send us a note in the **SUGGEST A TITLE** form on www.packtpub.com or e-mail suggest@packtpub.com.

If there is a topic that you have expertise in and you are interested in either writing or contributing to a book, see our author guide on www.packtpub.com/authors.

Customer support

Now that you are the proud owner of a Packt book, we have a number of things to help you to get the most from your purchase.

Downloading the example code

You can download the example code files for all Packt books you have purchased from your account at http://www.packtpub.com. If you purchased this book elsewhere, you can visit http://www.packtpub.com/support and register to have the files e-mailed directly to you.

Errata

Although we have taken every care to ensure the accuracy of our content, mistakes do happen. If you find a mistake in one of our books—maybe a mistake in the text or the code—we would be grateful if you could report this to us. By doing so, you can save other readers from frustration and help us improve subsequent versions of this book. If you find any errata, please report them by visiting http://www.packtpub.com/submit-errata, selecting your book, clicking on the **Errata Submission Form** link, and entering the details of your errata. Once your errata are verified, your submission will be accepted and the errata will be uploaded to our website or added to any list of existing errata under the Errata section of that title.

To view the previously submitted errata, go to https://www.packtpub.com/books/content/support and enter the name of the book in the search field. The required information will appear under the **Errata** section.

Piracy

Piracy of copyright material on the Internet is an ongoing problem across all media. At Packt, we take the protection of our copyright and licenses very seriously. If you come across any illegal copies of our works, in any form, on the Internet, please provide us with the location address or website name immediately so that we can pursue a remedy.

Please contact us at copyright@packtpub.com with a link to the suspected pirated material.

We appreciate your help in protecting our authors, and our ability to bring you valuable content.

Questions

If you have a problem with any aspect of this book, you can contact us at questions@packtpub.com, and we will do our best to address the problem.

Getting Started with Meteor

Welcome to this book on Meteor. Meteor is an exciting new JavaScript framework, and we will soon see how easy it is to achieve real and impressive results with less code.

In this chapter, we will learn what the requirements are and what additional tools we need to get started. We will see how simple it is to get our first Meteor application running and what a good basic folder structure for a Meteor app could be. We will also learn about Meteor's automatic build process and its specific way of loading files.

We will also see how to add packages using Meteors official packaging system. At the end of the chapter, we will take a short look at Meteor's command-line tool and some of its functions.

To bring it together, we will cover the following topics:

- The full-stack framework of Meteor
- Meteor's requirements
- Installing Meteor
- Adding basic packages
- Meteor's folder conventions and loading order
- Meteor's command-line tool

The full-stack framework of Meteor

Meteor is not just a JavaScript library such as jQuery or AngularJS. It's a full-stack solution that contain frontend libraries, a Node.js-based server, and a command-line tool. All this together lets us write large-scale web applications in JavaScript, on both the server and client, using a consistent API.

Even with Meteor being quite young, already a few companies such as `https://lookback.io`, `https://respond.ly`, and `https://madeye.io` use Meteor in their production environment.

If you want to see for yourself what's made with Meteor, take a look at `http://madewith.meteor.com`.

Meteor makes it easy for us to build web applications quickly and takes care of the boring processes such as file linking, minifying, and concatenating of files.

Here are a few highlights of what is possible with Meteor:

- We can build complex web applications amazingly fast using templates that automatically update themselves when data changes
- We can push new code to all clients on the fly while they are using our app
- Meteor core packages come with a complete account solution, allowing a seamless integration of Facebook, Twitter, and more
- Data will automatically be synced across clients, keeping every client in the same state in almost real time
- Latency compensation will make our interface appear super fast while the server response happens in the background.

With Meteor, we never have to link files with the `<script>` tags in HTML. Meteor's command-line tool automatically collects JavaScript or CSS files in our application's folder and links them in the `index.html` file, which is served to clients on initial page load. This makes structuring our code in separate files as easy as creating them.

Meteor's command-line tool also watches all files inside our application's folder for changes and rebuilds them on the fly when they change.

Additionally, it starts a Meteor server that serves the app's files to the clients. When a file changes, Meteor reloads the site of every client while preserving its state. This is called a **hot code reload**.

In production, the build process also concatenates and minifies our CSS and JavaScript files.

By simply adding the `less` and `coffee` core packages, we can even write all styles in LESS and code in CoffeeScript with no extra effort.

The command-line tool is also the tool for deploying and bundling our app so that we can run it on a remote server.

Sounds awesome? Let's take a look at what's needed to use Meteor.

Meteor's requirements

Meteor is not just a JavaScript framework and server. As we saw earlier, it is also a command-line tool that has a whole build process for us in place.

Currently, the operating systems that are officially supported are as follows:

- Mac OS X 10.6 and above
- Linux x86 and x86_64 systems
- Windows

 The Windows installer is still in development at the time of writing this book. Please follow the wiki page at `https://github.com/meteor/meteor/wiki/Preview-of-Meteor-on-Windows`.

This book and all examples use *Meteor 1.0*.

Using Chrome's developer tools

We will also need Google Chrome or Firefox with the Firebug add-on installed to follow examples that require a console. The examples, screenshots, and explanations in this book will use Google Chrome's developer tools.

Using Git and GitHub

I highly recommend using **GitHub** when working with web projects, such as the one we will work on in this book. Git and GitHub help us to back up our progress and let us always go back to previous states while seeing what we've changed.

Git is a version control system, which was created in 2005 by the inventor of Linux, Linus Torvalds.

With Git, we can *commit* any state of our code and later go back to that exact state. It also allows multiple developers to work on the same code base and merge their results together in an automated process. If conflicts appear in this process, the merging developer is able to resolve those *merge conflicts* by removing the unwanted lines of code.

I also recommend registering an account at http://github.com, as this is the easiest way to browse our code history. They have an easy to use interface as well as a great Windows and Mac app.

To follow the code examples in this book, you can download all code examples for each chapter from the book's web page at https://www.packtpub.com/books/content/support/17713.

Additionally, you will be able to clone the book's code from http://github.com/frozeman/book-building-single-page-web-apps-with-meteor. Every tag in this repository equals to one chapter of the book and the commit history will help you to see the changes, which were made in each chapter.

Installing Meteor

Installing Meteor is as easy as running the following command in the terminal:

```
$ curl https://install.meteor.com/ | sh
```

That's it! This will install the Meteor command-line tool ($ meteor), the Meteor server, MongoDB database, and the Meteor core packages (libraries).

> All command-line examples are run and tested on Mac OS X and can differ on Linux or Windows systems.

Installing Git

To install Git, I recommend installing the GitHub app from https://mac.github.com or https://windows.github.com. We can then simply go inside the app to **Preferences** and click on the **Install Command Line Tools** button inside the **Advanced** tab.

If we want to install Git manually and set it up via the command line, we can download the Git installer from http://git-scm.com and follow this great guide at https://help.github.com/articles/set-up-git.

Now, we can check whether everything was installed successfully by opening the terminal and running the following command:

```
$ git
```

Downloading the example code

You can download the example code files for all Packt books you have purchased from your account at http://www.packtpub.com. If you purchased this book elsewhere, you can visit http://www.packtpub. com/support and register to have the files e-mailed directly to you.

This should return us a list of Git options. If we get command not found: git, we need to check whether the git binary was correctly added to our PATH environment variable.

If everything is fine, we are ready to create our first Meteor app.

Creating our first app

To create our first app, we open the terminal, go to the folder where we want to create our new project, and enter the following commands:

```
$ cd my/developer/folder
$ meteor create my-meteor-blog
```

Meteor will now create a folder named my-meteor-blog. The HTML, CSS, and JavaScript files that Meteor created for us inside this folder are already a fully working Meteor app. To see it in action, run the following commands:

```
$ cd my-meteor-blog
$ meteor
```

Meteor will now start a local server for us on port 3000. Now, we can open our web browser and navigate to http://localhost:3000. We will see the app running.

This app doesn't do much, except showing a simple reactive example. If you click on the **Click Me** button, it will increase the counter:

For later examples, we will need Google Chrome's developer tools. To open the console, we can press *Alt + command + I* on Mac OS X or click on the menu button on the upper-right corner of Chrome, select **More tools,** and then **Developer tools**.

The **Developer tools** allow us to inspect the DOM and CSS of our website, as well as having a console where we can interact with our website's JavaScript.

Creating a good folder structure

For this book, we will build our own app from scratch. This also means we have to set up a sustainable folder structure, which helps us to keep our code organized.

With Meteor, we are very flexible concerning our folder structure. This means we can put our files wherever we want, as long as they are inside the app's folder. Meteor treats specific folders differently, allowing us to expose files only on the client, the server, or both. We will take a look at those specific folders later.

But, first let's get our hands dirty by deleting all preadd files in our newly created application folder and creating the following folder structure:

```
- my-meteor-blog
   - server
   - client
      - styles
      - templates
```

Preadd style files

To fully focus on the Meteor code but still have a pretty-looking blog, I strongly recommend to download the code that accompanies this chapter from the book's web page at `http://packtpub.com/books/content/support/17713`. They will contain already two drop-in-place style files (`lesshat.import.less` and `styles.less`), which will let your example blog look pretty in the upcoming chapters.

You can also download these files directly from GitHub at `https://github.com/frozeman/book-building-single-page-web-apps-with-meteor/tree/chapter1/my-meteor-blog/client/styles` and copy them to the `my-meteor-blog/client/styles` folder manually.

Next, we need to add some basic packages so that we can start building our app.

Adding basic packages

Packages in Meteor are libraries that can be added to our projects. The nice thing about Meteor packages is that they are self-contained units, which run out of the box. They mostly add either some templating functionality or provide extra objects in the global namespace of our project.

Packages can also add features to Meteor's build process such as the `stylus` package, which lets us write our app's style files with the `stylus` preprocessor syntax.

For our blog, we will need two packages at first:

`less`: This is a Meteor core package and will compile our style files on the fly to CSS

`jeeeyul:moment-with-langs`: This is a third-party library for date parsing and formatting

Adding a core package

To add the `less` package, we can simply open the terminal, go to our projects folder, and enter the following command:

```
$ meteor add less
```

Now, we are able to use any `*.less` files in our project, and Meteor will automatically compile them in its build process for us.

Adding a third-party package

To add a third-party package, we can simply search for packages on either `https://atmospherejs.com`, which is the frontend for Meteors packaging system, or use the command-line tool, `$ meteor search <package name>`.

For our blog, we will need the `jeeeyul:moment-with-langs` package that allows us later to simply manipulate and format dates.

Packages are namespaced with the authors name followed by a colon.

To add the `moment` package, we simply enter the following command:

```
$ meteor add jeeeyul:moment-with-langs
```

After the process is done, and we restarted our app using `$ meteor`, we will have the `moment` object available in our app global namespace and we can make use of it in the upcoming chapters.

Should we ever want to add only specific version of a package, we can use the following command:

```
$ meteor add jeeeyul:moment-with-langs@=2.8.2
```

If you want a version in the 1.0.0 (but not the 2.0.0) range use the following command:

```
$ meteor add jeeeyul:moment-with-langs@1.0.0
```

To update only packages we can simply run the following command:

```
$ meteor update --packages-only
```

Additionally, we can update only a specific package using the following command:

```
$ meteor update jeeeyul:moment-with-langs
```

That's it! Now we are fully ready to start creating our first templates. You can jump right into the next chapter, but make sure you come back to read on, as we will now talk about Meteor's build process in more detail.

Variable scopes

To understand Meteor's build process and its folder conventions, we need to take a quick look at variable scopes.

Meteor wraps every code files in an anonymous function before serving it. Therefore, declaring a variable with the `var` keyword will make it only available in that file's scope, which means these variables can't be accessed in any other file of your app. However, when we declare a variable without this keyword, we make it a globally available variable, which means it can be accessed from any file in our app. To understand this, we can take a look at the following example:

```
// The following files content
var myLocalVariable = 'test';
myGlobalVariable = 'test';
```

After Meteor's build process, the preceding lines of code will be as follows:

```
(function(){
  var myLocalVariable = 'test';
  myGlobalVariable = 'test';
})();
```

This way, the variable created with *var* is a local variable of the anonymous function, while the other one can be accessed globally, as it could be created somewhere else before.

Meteor's folder conventions and loading order

Though Meteor doesn't impose restrictions concerning our folder names or structure, there are naming conventions that help Meteor's build process to determine the order in which the files need to be loaded.

The following table describes the folder and their specific loading order:

Folder name	Load behavior
client	This is loaded only on the client.
client/compatibility	This will not be wrapped in an anonymous function. This is made for libraries that declare top-level variables with `var`. Additionally, files in this folder will be loaded before other files on the client.
server	Files in this folder will only be served on the server.

Folder name	Load behavior
public	This folder can contain assets used on the client, such as images, favicon.ico, or robots.txt. Folders and files inside the public folder are available on the client from root, /.
private	This folder can contain assets that will only be available on the server. These files are available through Assets API.
lib	Files and subfolders inside a lib folder will be loaded before other files, where lib folders in deeper folders will be loaded before the files in lib folders of their parent folders.
tests	Files inside this folder won't be touched or loaded by Meteor at all.
packages	When we want to use local packages, we can add them to this folder and Meteor will use those packages, even if one with the same name exists in Meteor's official package system. (However, we still have to add the packages using $ meteor add . . . .)

The following table describes filenames that have created a specific loading order:

Filename	Load behavior
main.*	Files with this name are loaded last, whereas files in deeper folders are loaded before the files of their parent folders
.	Files outside of the former mentioned folders in this table are loaded on both the client and server

So, we see that Meteor gathers all files except the ones inside public, private, and tests.

Additionally, files are always loaded in the alphabetical order, and files in subfolders are loaded before the ones in parent folders.

If we have files outside the client or server folder and want to determine where the code should be executed, we can use the following variables:

```
if(Meteor.isClient) {
  // Some code executed on the client
}

if(Meteor.isServer) {
```

```
  // Some code executed on the server.
}
```

We also see that code inside a `main.*` file is loaded last. To make sure a specific code only loads when all files are loaded and the DOM on the client is ready, we can use the Meteor's `startup()` function:

```
Meteor.startup(function(){
  /*
  This code runs on the client when the DOM is ready,
  and on the server when the server process is finished starting.
  */
});
```

Loading assets on the server

To load files from inside the `private` folder on the server, we can use the `Assets` API as follows:

```
Assets.getText(assetPath, [asyncCallback]);
// or
Assets.getBinary(assetPath, [asyncCallback])
```

Here, `assetPath` is a file path relative to the `private` folder, for example, `'subfolder/data.txt'`.

If we provide a callback function as the second parameter, the `Assets()` method will run asynchronously. So, we have two ways of retrieving the content of an assets file:

```
// Synchronously
var myData = Assets.getText('data.txt');

// Or asynchronously
Assets.getText('data.txt', function(error, result){
  // Do somthing with the result.
  // If the error parameter is not NULL, something went wrong
});
```

 If the first example returns an error, our current server code will fail. In the second example, our code will still work, as the error is contained in the `error` parameter.

Now that we understand Meteor's basic folder structure, let's take a brief look at the Meteor's command-line tool.

Meteor's command-line tool

Now that we know already about Meteor's build process and folder structure, we will take a closer look at what we can do with the command-line tool that Meteor provides.

As we saw when using the `meteor` command, we need to be inside a Meteor project so that all actions will be performed on this project. For example, when we run `meteor add xxx`, we add a package to the project where we are currently in.

Updating Meteor

If Meteor releases a new version, we can simply update our project by running the following command:

```
$ meteor update
```

If we want to go back to a previous version, we can do this by running the following command:

```
$ meteor update --release 0.9.1
```

This would set our project back to release version 0.9.1.

Deploying Meteor

Deploying our Meteor app to a public server is as easy as running the following command:

```
$ meteor deploy my-app-name
```

This would ask us to register a Meteor developer account and deploy our app at `http://my-app-name.meteor.com`.

For a full introduction on how to deploy a Meteor app, refer to *Chapter 10, Deploying Our App*.

In the *Appendix*, you can find a full list of Meteor commands and their explanations.

Summary

In this chapter, we learned what Meteor requires to run, how to create a Meteor application, and how the build process works.

We understand that Meteor's folder structure is rather flexible, but that there are special folders such as the `client`, `server`, and `lib` folder, which are loaded in different places and order. We also saw how to add packages and how to use the Meteor command-line tool.

If you want to dig deeper into what we've learned so far, take a look at the following parts of the Meteor documentation:

- `https://www.meteor.com/projects`
- `https://www.meteor.com/tool`
- `https://docs.meteor.com/#/full/whatismeteor`
- `https://docs.meteor.com/#/full/structuringyourapp`
- `https://docs.meteor.com/#/full/usingpackages`
- `https://docs.meteor.com/#/full/assets`
- `https://docs.meteor.com/#/full/commandline`

You can find this chapter's code examples at `https://www.packtpub.com/books/content/support/17713` or on GitHub at `https://github.com/frozeman/book-building-single-page-web-apps-with-meteor/tree/chapter1`.

Now that we've set up our project's basic folder structure, we are ready to start with the fun part of Meteor — templates.

2

Building HTML Templates

After we successfully installed Meteor and set up our folder structure, we can now start building the basic templates for our blog.

In this chapter, we will learn how templates are built. We will see how to display data and how some parts can be altered using helper functions. We will take a look on adding events, using conditions, and understanding data contexts, all in templates.

The following is an overview of what will be covered in this chapter:

- The basic template structure
- Displaying data
- Writing template helper functions
- Using conditions in templates
- Data contexts and how those can be set
- Nesting templates and data context inheritance
- Adding events
- Building block helpers

If you jump right into this chapter without setting up the folder structure in the *Chapter 1, Getting Started with Meteor*, download the previous chapter's code examples from either the book's web page at `https://www.packtpub.com/books/content/support/17713` or from the GitHub repository at `https://github.com/frozeman/book-building-single-page-web-apps-with-meteor/tree/chapter1`.

These code examples will also contain all the style files, so we don't have to worry about adding CSS code along the way.

Writing templates in Meteor

Normally when we build websites, we build the complete HTML on the server side. This was quite straightforward; every page is built on the server, then it is sent to the client, and at last JavaScript added some additional animation or dynamic behavior to it.

This is not so in single-page apps, where every page needs to be already in the client's browser so that it can be shown at will. Meteor solves this problem by providing templates that exists in JavaScript and can be placed in the DOM at some point. These templates can have nested templates, allowing for an easy way to reuse and structure an app's HTML layout.

Since Meteor is so flexible in terms of folder and file structure, any `*.html` page can contain a template and will be parsed during Meteor's build process. This allows us to put all templates in the `my-meteor-blog/client/templates` folder, which we created in the *Chapter 1, Getting Started with Meteor*. This folder structure is chosen as it helps us organizing templates when our app grows.

Meteor's template engine is called **Spacebars**, which is a derivative of the handlebars template engine. Spacebars is built on top of **Blaze**, which is Meteor's reactive DOM update engine.

Blaze can generate reactive HTML directly using its API, though it's more convenient to use Meteor's Spacebars or a third-party template language built on top of Blaze such as Jade for Meteor.

For more detail about Blaze, visit `https://docs.meteor.com/#/full/blaze` and `https://github.com/mquandalle/meteor-jade`.

What makes Spacebars so exciting is its simplicity and reactivity. Reactive templates mean that some parts of the template can automatically change when the underlying data changes. There is no need of manual DOM manipulation and inconsistent interfaces belong to the past. To get a better understanding of Meteor, we will start with the basic HTML files for our app:

1. Let's create an `index.html` file in our `my-meteor-blog/client` folder with the following lines of code:

    ```
    <head>
      <title>My Meteor Blog</title>
    </head>
    <body>
      Hello World
    </body>
    ```

Note that our `index.html` file doesn't contain the `<html>...</html>` tags, as Meteor gathers all `<head>` and `<body>` tags in any file and builds up its own `index.html` file, which will be delivered to the user. Actually, we can also name this file `myapp.html`.

2. Next, we run our Meteor app from the command line by typing the following command:

```
$ cd my-meteor-blog
$ meteor
```

This will start a Meteor server with our app running.

3. That's it! We can open our browser, navigate to `http://localhost:3000`, and we should see **Hello World**.

What happens here is that Meteor will look through all the HTML files available in our app's folder, concatenating the content of all `<head>` and `<body>` tags, which it finds and serve them to the clients as its index file.

If we take a look at the source code of our app, we will see that the `<body>` tag is empty. This is because Meteor sees the content of the `<body>` tag as its own templates, which will be injected with its corresponding JavaScript template when the DOM is loaded.

 To see the source code, don't use the Developer Tools' **elements panel**, as this will show us the source code after the JavaScript is executed. Right-click on the website instead and select **View page source** in Chrome.

We will also see that Meteor already linked all kinds of JavaScript files in our `<head>` tag. These are Meteor's core packages and our add third-party packages. In production, these files will be concatenated into one. To see this in action, go to the terminal, quit our running Meteor server using *Ctrl + C*, and run the following command:

```
$ meteor --production
```

If we now take a look at the source code, we will see that there is only one cryptic-looking JavaScript file linked.

For the next steps, it is better to go back to our developer mode by simply quitting Meteor and running the `meteor` command again, since this will reload the app faster when file changes occur.

Building the basic templates

Now, let's add the basic templates to our blog by creating a file called layout.html in the my-meteor-blog/client/templates folder. This template will serve as the wrapper template for our blog layout. To build the basic templates, perform the following steps:

1. Add the following lines of code to layout.html, which we just created:

```
<template name="layout">
  <header>
    <div class="container">
      <h1>My Meteor Single Page App</h1>
      <ul>
        <li>
          <a href="/">Home</a>
        </li>
        <li>
          <a href="/about">About</a>
        </li>
      </ul>
    </div>
  </header>

  <div class="container">
    <main>
    </main>
  </div>
</template>
```

2. Next, we will create the home page template, which will later list all our blogs posts. In the same templates folder as layout.html, we will create a file named home.html with the following lines of code:

```
<template name="home">
{{#markdown}}
## Welcome to my Blog
Here I'm talking about my latest discoveries from the world of
JavaScript.
{{/markdown}}
</template>
```

3. The next file will be a simple **About** page and we save it as about.html with the following code snippet:

```
<template name="about">
{{#markdown}}
## About me
```

```
Lorem ipsum dolor sit amet, consectetur adipisicing elit, sed do
eiusmod
tempor incididunt ut labore et dolore magna aliqua. Ut enim ad
minim veniam,
quis nostrud **exercitation ullamco** laboris nisi ut aliquip ex
ea commodo
consequat.

Link to my facebook: [facebook.com][1]

[1]: http://facebook.com
{{/markdown}}
</template>
```

As you can see, we used a {{#markdown}} block helper to wrap our texts. The curly braces are handlebars syntax, which Blaze uses to bring logic to the HTML. The {{#markdown}}...{{/markdown}} block will transform all markdown syntax inside into HTML when the template gets rendered.

 The markdown text cannot be indented as we do with the HTML tags because the markdown syntax interprets indentation as code.

4. To be able to use {{#markdown}} block helper, we need to first add the markdown core package to our app. To do this, we quit our running app in the terminal using *Ctrl + C* and type the following command:

   $ meteor add markdown

5. Now we can run the meteor command again to start our server.

However, when we now go to our browser, we will still see **Hello World**. So how can we make now our templates visible?

Adding templates and partials

To show the home template in the app, we need to open index.html, which we created earlier, and perform the following steps:

1. We replace Hello World with the following template inclusion helper:

   {{> layout}}

2. If we go back to our browser now, we see that the text is gone and the layout template, which we created earlier, has appeared with its header and menu.

---

3. To complete the page, we need to show the home template in the layout template. We do this by simply adding another template inclusion helper to the main section of the layout template in our layout.html file, as follows:

```
<main>
  {{> home}}
</main>
```

4. If we go back to the browser, we should see the following screenshot:

If we would now switch {{> home}} for {{> about}}, we would see our about template instead.

Displaying data with template helpers

Each template can have functions, which are called template helpers, and they can be used inside the template and child templates.

In addition to our custom helper functions, there are three callback functions that are called when the template is created, rendered, and destroyed. To display data with template helpers, perform the following steps:

1. To see the three callback functions in action, let's create a file called home.js and save it to our my-meteor-blog/client/templates/ folder with the following code snippet:

```
Template.home.created = function(){
  console.log('Created the home template');
};
```

```
Template.home.rendered = function(){
  console.log('Rendered the home template');
};

Template.home.destroyed = function(){
  console.log('Destroyed the home template');
};
```

If we now open the console of our browser, we will see the first two callbacks are being fired. The last one will only fire if we dynamically remove the template.

2. To display data in the home template, we will create a helper function that will return a simple string as follows:

```
Template.home.helpers({
  exampleHelper: function(){
    return 'This text came from a helper with some <strong>HTML</strong>.';
  }
});
```

3. Now if we go to our home.html file, add the {{exampleHelper}} helper after the {{markdown}} block helper, and save the file, we will see the string appearing in our browser, but we will notice that the HTML is escaped.

4. To make Meteor render the HTML correctly, we can simply replace the double curly braces with triple curly braces, as shown in the following line of code, and Blaze won't let the HTML escape:

```
{{{exampleHelper}}}
```

> Note that in most of our templates helper, we *shouldn't* use triple stache {{{...}}} as this opens the door for XSS and other attacks. Only use it if the HTML returned is safe to be rendered.

5. Additionally, we can return unescaped HTML using double curly braces, but we need to return the string passed through the SpaceBars.SafeString function, as shown in the following example:

```
Template.home.helpers({
  exampleHelper: function(){
    return new Spacebars.SafeString('This text came from a helper with some <strong>HTML</strong>.');
  }
});
```

Setting the data context for a template

Now that we've seen how we can display data using a helper, let's see how we can set the whole data context of a template:

1. For the next examples, we will create a file called `examples.html` in our `my-meteor-blog/client/templates` folder and add the following code snippet:

```
<template name="contextExample">
  <p>{{someText}}</p>
</template>
```

2. Now that we have our `contextExample` template, we can add it to our `home` template by passing some data as follows:

```
{{> contextExample someText="I was set in the parent template's
helper, as an argument."}}
```

This will show the text in the `contextExample` template because we were displaying it using `{{someText}}`.

 Remember that filenames don't really matter as Meteor is collecting and concatenating them anyway; however, the template name matters since we use this to reference templates.

Setting the context in HTML is not very dynamic, as it is hardcoded. To be able to dynamically change the context, it is better to set it using a `template` helper function.

3. To do this, we must first add the helper to our `home` templates helpers, which returns the data context, as follows:

```
Template.home.helpers({
  // other helpers ...
  dataContextHelper: function(){
    return {
      someText: 'This text was set using a helper of the parent
template.',
      someNested: {
        text: 'That comes from "someNested.text"'
      }
    };
  }
});
```

4. Now we can add this helper as the data context to our `contextExample` template inclusion helper, as follows:

```
{{> contextExample dataContextHelper}}
```

5. Also, to show the nested data object we return, we can use Blaze dot syntax in the `contextExample` template by adding the following line of code to the template:

```
<p>{{someNested.text}}</p>
```

This will now display both the `someText` and the `someNested.text`, which was returned by our helper functions.

Using the {{#with}} block helper

Another way of setting the data context is by using the {{#with}} block helper. The following code snippet has the same result as the former inclusion helper that utilizes the helper function:

```
{{#with dataContextHelper}}
  {{> contextExample}}
{{/with}}
```

We would even get the same results in the browser when we don't use a subtemplate and just add the content of the `contextExample` template inside the {{#with}} block helper, as follows:

```
{{#with dataContextHelper}}
  <p>{{someText}}</p>
  <p>{{someNested.text}}</p>
{{/with}}
```

"this" in template helpers and template callbacks

In Meteor, `this` in template helpers is used differently in template callbacks such as `created()`, `rendered()`, and `destroyed()`.

As already mentioned, templates have three callback functions that are fired in different states of the template:

- `created`: This fires when the template gets initiated but is not yet in the DOM

- `rendered`: This fires when the template and all its sub templates are attached to the DOM
- `destroyed`: This fires when the template is removed from the DOM and before the instance of the template gets destroyed

In these callback functions, `this` refers to the current template instance. The instance object can access the templates DOM and comes with the following methods:

- `this.$(selectorString)`: This method finds all elements that match `selectorString` and returns a jQuery object from those elements.
- `this.findAll(selectorString)`: This method finds all elements that match `selectorString`, but returns the plain DOM elements.
- `this.find(selectorString)`: This method finds the first element that matches `selectorString` and returns a plain DOM element.
- `this.firstNode`: This object contains the first element in the template.
- `this.lastNode`: This object contains the last element in the template.
- `this.data`: This object contains the templates data context
- `this.autorun(runFunc)`: A reactive `Tracker.autorun()` function that is stopped when the template instance is destroyed.
- `this.view`: This object contains the `Blaze.View` instance for this template. `Blaze.View` are the building blocks of reactive templates.

Inside helper functions, `this` refers only to the current data context.

To make these different behaviors visible, we will take a look at some examples:

- When we want to access the DOM of a template, we must do it in the rendered callback because only at this point, the template elements will be in the DOM. To see it in action, we edit our `home.js` file as follows:

```
Template.home.rendered = function(){
  console.log('Rendered the home template');

  this.$('p').html('We just replaced that text!');
};
```

  This will replace the first p tag that is created by the {{#markdown}} block helper, which we put there before, with the string we set. Now when we check the browser, we will see that the first <p> tag that contained our blog's introduction text has been replaced.

- For the next example, we need to create an additional template JavaScript file for our `contextExample` template. To do this, we create a new file called `examples.js` in our `templates` folder and save it using the following code snippet:

```
Template.contextExample.rendered = function(){
  console.log('Rendered Context Example', this.data);
};

Template.contextExample.helpers({
  logContext: function(){
    console.log('Context Log Helper', this);
  }
});
```

  This will add the rendered callback as well as a helper called `logContext` to our `contextExample` template helpers. To make this helper run, we also need to add this helper to our `contextExample` template as follows:

```
<p>{{logContext}}</p>
```

When we now go back to the console of our browser, we see that the data context object has been returned for all the `rendered` callbacks and helpers from our rendered `contextTemplates` template. We can also see that helpers will run before the rendered callback.

 In case you need access to the templates instance from inside a template helper, you can use `Template.instance()` to get it.

Now let's use make our template interactive using events.

Adding events

To make our template a bit more dynamic, we will add a simple event, which will reactively rerun the `logContext` helper we created earlier.

First, however, we need to add a button to our `contextExample` template:

```
<button>Get some random number</button>
```

To catch the click event, open `examples.js` and add the following event function:

```
Template.contextExample.events({
  'click button': function(e, template){
    Session.set('randomNumber', Math.random(0,99));
  }
});
```

This will set a session variable called randomNumber to a random number.

 We will talk in depth about sessions in the next chapter. For now, we only need to know that when a session variable changes, all functions that get that session variable using Session.get('myVariable') will run again.

To see this in action, we will add a Session.get() call to the logContext helper, and return the former set's random number as follows:

```
Template.contextExample.helpers({
  logContext: function(){
    console.log('Context Log Helper',this);

    return Session.get('randomNumber');
  }
});
```

If we go to the browser, we will see the **Get some random number** button. When we click on it, we see a random number appearing just above the button.

 When we use the contextTemplates template multiple times in our home template, we will see that each instance of that template helper will display the same random number. This is because the session object will rerun all its dependencies, all of which are instances of the logHelper helper.

Now that we have covered template helpers, let's create a custom block helper.

Block helpers

Block helpers are templates that wrap the content of the block. They can be used to show content in different ways depending on conditions, or they can be used to add extra functionality to the blocks content, for example, some JavaScript calculation on its DOM elements.

In the following example, we will build a simple block helper that will show content based on a Boolean condition.

To do this, we will to add the following code snippet at the end of our example.html file:

```
<template name="blockHelperExample">
  <div>
```

```
    <h1>My Block Helper</h1>
    {{#if this}}
      <p>Content goes here: {{> Template.contentBlock}}</p>
    {{else}}
      <p>Else content here: {{> Template.elseBlock}}</p>
    {{/if}}
  </div>
</template>
```

The `{{> Template.contentBlock}}` is a predefined placeholder for the block's content. The same applies for `{{> Template.elseBlock}}`.

When `this` (in this example, we use the template's context as a simple Boolean) is `true`, it will show the given `Template.contentBlock`. Otherwise, it will show the `Template.elseBlock` content.

To see how we can use the recently created template as a block helper, take a look at the following example, which we can add to `home` template:

```
{{#blockHelperExample true}}
  <span>Some Content</span>
{{else}}
  <span>Some Warning</span>
{{/blockHelperExample}}
```

Now we should see the following screenshot:

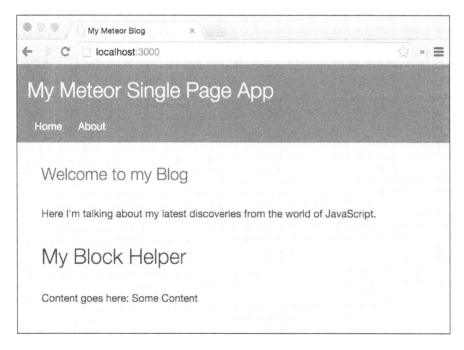

When we now change `true`, which we pass to `{{#blockHelperExample}}`, to `false`, we should see the content after the `{{else}}` instead.

We can also use a helper function to replace the Boolean value, so that we can switch the block helper dynamically. Additionally, we can pass key-value arguments and access them by their key inside the block helper template, as shown in the following code example:

```
{{#blockHelperExample myValue=true}}
...
{{/blockHelperExample}}
```

We can also access the given argument by its name in the block template as follows:

```
<template name="blockHelperExample">
  <div>
    <h1>My Block Helper</h1>
    {{#if myValue}}
    ...
    {{/if}}
  </div>
</template>
```

 Note that the data context for the block's content will be the one from the template in which the block appears, not the one of the block helper template itself.

Block helpers are a powerful tool because they allow us to write self-contained components that, when packed into a package, can be used as a drop-in-place functionality by others. This feature has the potential to allow for a vibrant marketplace, like the marketplace we see in jQuery plugins.

Listing posts

Now that we have walked through all ways of using helpers and data, I want to introduce a block helper named `{{#each}}`, which we will probably find the most useful.

If we go through all the examples completed up to now, we can see that it is better to delete all the examples of data context from our `home` template, the `examples.html` file, and its `examples.js` JavaScript file so that we can continue to build our blog cleanly.

The next step is to add a list of blog entries to our home page. For this, we need to create a template for a post preview. This can be done by performing the following steps:

1. We create a file called `postInList.html` in our `my-meteor-blog/client/templates` folder and save it with the following code snippet:

    ```
    <template name="postInList">
      <div class="postListItem">
        <h2><a href="#">{{title}}</a></h2>
        <p>{{description}}</p>
        <div class="footer">
          Posted by {{author}}
        </div>
      </div>
    </template>
    ```

    This template will be used for each post we display in the home page.

2. To make it appear, we need to add a `{{#each}}` helper to the `home` template, as follows:

    ```
    {{#each postsList}}
      {{> postInList}}
    {{/each}}
    ```

    When the `postsList` helper, which we pass to the `{{#each}}` block helper, returns an array, the content of `{{#each}}` will be repeated for each item in the array, setting the array item as the data context.

3. To see this in action, we add the `postsList` helper in our `home.js` file to the template helpers, as follows:

    ```
    Template.home.helpers({
      // other helpers ...
      postsList: function(){
        return [
          {
            title: 'My Second entry',
            description: 'Borem sodum color sit amet, consetetur
    sadipscing elitr.',
            author: 'Fabian Vogelsteller',
            timeCreated: moment().subtract(3, 'days').unix()
          },
          {
            title: 'My First entry',
    ```

```
        description: 'Lorem ipsum dolor sit amet, consetetur
sadipscing elitr.',
        author: 'Fabian Vogelsteller',
        timeCreated: moment().subtract(7, 'days').unix()
      }
    ];
  }
});
```

4. As we can see, we return an array where each item is an object containing our post's data context. For `timeCreated`, we use the `moment` function of our previously added third-party package. This will generate dummy timestamps of a few days in the past. If we now go to our browser, we will see the two posts listed, as shown in the following screenshot:

5. To display `timeCreated` from our post item in the correct format, we need to create a helper function to format the timestamp. However, because we want to use this helper in other templates later, we need to make it a global helper that can be accessed by any template. To do this, we create a file named `template-helpers.js` and save it to our `my-meteor-blog/client` folder, as it doesn't belonging to any specific template.

6. To register a global helper, we can use Meteor's `Template.registerHelper` function:

```
Template.registerHelper('formatTime', function(time, type){
  switch(type){
    case 'fromNow':
      return moment.unix(time).fromNow();
    case 'iso':
      return moment.unix(time).toISOString();
    default:
      return moment.unix(time).format('LLLL');
  }
});
```

7. Now, we only have to add the helper to our `postInList` template by replacing the content of the footer with the following code snippet:

```
<div class="footer">
  <time datetime="{{formatTime timeCreated "iso"}}">Posted
    {{formatTime timeCreated "fromNow"}} by {{author}}</time>
</div>
```

Now, if we save both the files and go back to our browser, we will see a relative date added to our blog post's footer. This works because we pass the time and a type string to the helper, as follows:

```
{{formatTime timeCreated "fromNow"}}
```

The helper then returns the formatted date using a `moment` function.

With this global helper, we can now format any Unix timestamp, in any template to relative times, ISO time strings, and a standard date format (using the LLLL format, which converts to Thursday, September 4, 1986, 8:30 P.M.).

Now that we have already used the `{{#with}}` and `{{#each}}` block helpers, let's take a look at the other default helpers and syntax that Blaze uses.

Spacebars syntax

To wrap it all up, lets summarize the Spacebars syntax:

Helper	Description
`{{myProperty}}`	The template helper can be a property from the template's data context or a template helper function. If a helper function and a property with the same name exist, the template helper will use the helper function instead.
`{{> myTemplate}}`	The inclusion helper is for a template and always expects a template object or null.
`{{> Template.dynamic template=templateName [data=dataContext]}}`	With the `{{> Template.dynamic ...}}` helper, you can render a template dynamically by providing a template helper returning a template name for the template parameter. When the helper would rerun and return a different template name, it will replace the template on this position with the new one.

`{{#myBlockHelper}}`
 ...
 `{{/myBlockHelper}}`
	A block helper that contains both HTML and the Spacebars syntax.

By default, Spacebars comes with the following four default block helpers:

- `{{#if}}..{{/if}}`
- `{{#unless}}..{{/unless}}`
- `{{#with}}..{{/with}}`
- `{{#each}}..{{/each}}`

The `{{#if}}` block helper allows us to create simple conditions, as follows:

```
{{#if myHelperWhichReturnsABoolean}}
  <h1>Show me this</h1>
{{else}}
  <strong>If not<strong> show this.
{{/if}}
```

The `{{#unless}}` block helper works the same as `{{#if}}`, but with swapped logic.

The `{{#with}}` block, as seen earlier, will set a new data context to its content and containing templates, and the `{{#each}}` block helper will render multiple times, setting a different data context for each iteration.

Accessing parent data contexts

To complete our journey through the Spacebars syntax, let's take a closer look at the template helper syntax that we used to display data. As we've already seen, we can display data using the double curly braces syntax, as follows:

```
{{myData}}
```

Inside this helper, we can access the properties of an object using the dot syntax:

```
{{myObject.myString}}
```

We can also access a parent data context using a path-like syntax:

```
{{../myParentsTemplateProperty}}
```

Additionally, we can move more than just one context up:

```
{{../../someParentProperty}}
```

This feature allows us to be very flexible about the data context.

> If we want to do the same from inside a template helper, we can use the Template API `Template.parentData(n)`, where n is the number of steps up to access the data context of parent templates.
>
> `Template.parentData(0)` is the same as `Template.currentData()`, or `this` if we are in a template helper.

Passing data to helpers

Passing data to helpers can be done in two different ways. We can pass arguments to a helper as follows:

```
{{myHelper "A String" aContextProperty}}
```

Then, we can access it in the helper as follows:

```
Template.myTemplate.helpers({
    myHelper: function(myString, myObject){
      // And we get:
      // myString = 'aString'
      // myObject = aContextProperty
    }
});
```

Besides this, we can pass data in the form of key-values:

```
{{myHelper myString="A String" myObject=aDataProperty}}
```

This time, however, we need to access them as follows:

```
Template.myTemplate.helpers({
    myHelper: function(Parameters){
      // And we can access them:
      // Parameters.hash.myString = 'aString'
      // Parameters.hash.myObject = aDataProperty
    }
});
```

Be aware that block and inclusion helpers act differently because they always expect objects or key-values as arguments:

```
{{> myTemplate someString="I will be available inside the template"}}


// Or


{{> myTemplate objectWithData}}
```

If we want to pass only a single variable or value to an inclusion or block helper, Meteor would objectify the argument, as we can see with the following code snippet:

```
{{#myBlock "someString"}}
...
{{/myBlock}}
```

We would then need to typecast the passed argument if we want to use it in a helper function as follows:

```
Template.myBlock.helpers({
    doSomethingWithTheString: function(){
      // Use String(this), to get the string
      return this;
    }
});
```

Beisdes, we can also simply display the string in our block helper template using `{{Template.contentBlock}}` as follows:

```
<template name="myBlock">
  <h1>{{this}}</h1>
  {{Template.contentBlock}}
</template>
```

We can also pass another template helper as an argument to an inclusion or block helper, as shown in the following example:

```
{{> myTemplate myHelperWhichReturnsAnObject "we pass a string and a
number" 300}}
```

Though passing data to template helpers and inclusion/block helpers are slightly different, arguments can be quite flexible when using helpers to generate them.

Summary

Reactive templates are one of the most impressive features of Meteor, and once we get used to them, we probably won't look back to manual DOM manipulation anymore.

After reading this chapter, we should know how to write and use templates in Meteor. We should also understand its basic syntax and how to add templates.

We saw how to access and set data in templates and how to use helpers. We learned about different types of helpers, such as inclusion helpers and block helpers. We also built our own custom block helpers and used Meteor's default helpers.

We learned that templates have three different callbacks, for when the template gets created, rendered, and destroyed.

We learned how to pass data to helpers, and how this differs in normal helpers and block helpers.

To dig deeper, take a look at the following documentations:

- https://docs.meteor.com/#/full/templates_api
- https://www.meteor.com/blaze
- https://docs.meteor.com/#/full/blaze
- https://atmospherejs.com/meteor/spacebars
- http://momentjs.com

You can find this chapter's code examples either at https://www.packtpub.com/books/content/support/17713 or on GitHub at https://github.com/frozeman/book-building-single-page-web-apps-with-meteor/tree/chapter2.

With all this new knowledge about templates, we are ready to add data to our database and see how we can display it in our home page.

3
Storing Data and Handling Collections

In the previous chapter, we learned how to build templates and display data in them. We built the basic layout of our app and listed some post examples on the front page.

In this chapter, we will add post examples persistently to our database on the server. We will learn how we can access this data later on the client and how Meteor syncs data between clients and the server.

In this chapter, we'll cover the following topics:

- Storing of data in Meteor
- Cresting collections
- Adding data to a collection
- Querying data from a collection
- Updating data in a collection
- What "database everywhere" means
- The difference between the server's and the client's databases

If you've jumped right into the chapter and want to follow the examples, download the previous chapter's code examples from either the book's web page at https://www.packtpub.com/books/content/support/17713 or from the GitHub repository at https://github.com/frozeman/book-building-single-page-web-apps-with-meteor/tree/chapter2.

These code examples will also contain all the style files, so we don't have to worry about adding CSS code along the way.

Meteor and databases

Meteor currently uses MongoDB by default to store data on the server, although there are drivers planned for use with relational databases too.

 If you are adventurous, you can try one of the community-built SQL drivers, such as the `numtel:mysql` package from `https://atmospherejs.com/numtel/mysql`.

MongoDB is a NoSQL database. This means it is based on a flat document structure instead of a relational table structure. Its document approach makes it ideal for JavaScript as documents are written in BJSON, which is very similar to the JSON format.

Meteor has a *database everywhere* approach, which means that we have the same API to query the database on the client as well as on the server. Yet, when we query the database on the client, we are only able to access the data that we *published* to a client.

MongoDB uses a data structure called **collection**, which is the equivalent of a table in a SQL database. Collections contain documents, where each document has its own unique ID. These documents are JSON-like structures and can contain properties with values, even with multiple dimensions, as follows:

```
{
  "_id": "W7sBzpBbov48rR7jW",
  "myName": "My Document Name",
  "someProperty": 123456,
  "aNestedProperty": {
    "anotherOne": "With another string"
  }
}
```

These collections are used to store data in the server's MongoDB as well as the client-side `minimongo` collection, which is an in-memory database mimicking the behavior of the real MongoDB.

 We'll discuss more about `minimongo` at the end of this chapter.

The MongoDB API allows us to use a simple JSON-based query language to get documents from a collection. We can pass additional options to only ask for *specific fields* or *sort* the returned documents. These are very powerful features, especially on the client side, to display data in various ways.

Setting up a collection

To see all this in action, let's get right on it by creating our first collection.

We create a file called `collections.js` inside our `my-meteor-blog` folder. We need to create it in the root folder so that it will be available on both the client and the server. Now let's add the following line of code to the `collections.js` file:

```
Posts = new Mongo.Collection('posts');
```

This will make the `Posts` variable globally available, as we haven't used the `var` keyword, which would restrict it to the scope of this file.

`Mongo.Collection` is the API used to query the database and it comes with the following basic methods:

- `insert`: This method is used to insert documents into the database
- `update`: This method is used to update documents or parts of them
- `upsert`: This method is used to insert or update documents or parts of them
- `remove`: This method is used to delete documents from the database
- `find`: This method is used to query the database for documents
- `findOne`: This method is used to return only the first matched document

Adding post examples

To query the database for posts, we need to add some post examples. This has to be done on the server, as we want to add them persistently. To add an example post, perform the following steps:

1. We create a file called `main.js` inside our `my-meteor-blog/server` folder. Inside this file, we will use the `Meteor.startup()` function to execute the code on the start of the server.

2. We then add the post example, but only when the collection is empty. So to prevent this, we add them every time we restart the server, as follows:

```
Meteor.startup(function(){

    console.log('Server started');

    // #Storing Data -> Adding post examples
    if(Posts.find().count() === 0) {

        console.log('Adding dummy posts');
```

```
var dummyPosts = [
  {
    title: 'My First entry',
    slug: 'my-first-entry',
    description: 'Lorem ipsum dolor sit amet.',
    text: 'Lorem ipsum dolor sit amet...',
    timeCreated: moment().subtract(7,'days').unix(),
    author: 'John Doe'
  },
  {
    title: 'My Second entry',
    slug: 'my-second-entry',
    description: 'Borem ipsum dolor sit.',
    text: 'Lorem ipsum dolor sit amet...',
    timeCreated: moment().subtract(5,'days').unix(),
    author: 'John Doe'
  },
  {
    title: 'My Third entry',
    slug: 'my-third-entry',
    description: 'Dorem ipsum dolor sit amet.',
    text: 'Lorem ipsum dolor sit amet...',
    timeCreated: moment().subtract(3,'days').unix(),
    author: 'John Doe'
  },
  {
    title: 'My Fourth entry',
    slug: 'my-fourth-entry',
    description: 'Sorem ipsum dolor sit amet.',
    text: 'Lorem ipsum dolor sit amet...',
    timeCreated: moment().subtract(2,'days').unix(),
    author: 'John Doe'
  },
  {
    title: 'My Fifth entry',
    slug: 'my-fifth-entry',
    description: 'Korem ipsum dolor sit amet.',
    text: 'Lorem ipsum dolor sit amet...',
    timeCreated: moment().subtract(1,'days').unix(),
    author: 'John Doe'
  }
];
```

```
    // we add the dummyPosts to our database
    _.each(dummyPosts, function(post){
      Posts.insert(post);
    });
  }
});
```

Now, when check out the terminal, we should see something similar to the following screenshot:

```
● ● ●                    2. meteor (mongod)
→ my-meteor-blog  meteor
[[[[ ~/Dropbox/Documents/Writing Single Page Apps using Meteor/Book - 1st Draft
/Chapter 3 rewritten/Code/my-meteor-blog ]]]]

=> Started proxy.
=> Started MongoDB.
I20141105-14:30:52.747(1)? Server started
I20141105-14:30:53.054(1)? Adding dummy posts
=> Started your app.

=> App running at: http://localhost:3000/
```

We can also add dummy data using the Mongo console instead of writing it in our code.

To use the Mongo console, we start the Meteor server using $ meteor, and then in a second terminal we run $ meteor mongo, which brings us to a Mongo shell.

Here, we can simply add documents using MongoDB's syntax:

```
db.posts.insert({title: 'My First entry',
  slug: 'my-first-entry',
  description: 'Lorem ipsum dolor sit amet.',
  text: 'Lorem ipsum dolor sit amet...',
  timeCreated: 1405065868,
  author: 'John Doe'
})
```

Querying a collection

The server did restart when we saved our changes. At this point, Meteor added five post examples to our database.

 If the server didn't restart, it means that we made a mistake in the syntax somewhere in our code. When we manually reload our browser or check out the terminal, we will see the error that Meteor gives us and we can fix it.

In case we messed up something in the database, we can always reset it using the $ `meteor reset` command in the terminal.

We can see these posts by simply opening up the console in our browser and typing the following command:

```
Posts.find().fetch();
```

This will return an array with five items, each of them being one of our example posts.

To list these newly inserted posts in our front page, we need to replace the content of our `postsList` helper in the `home.js` file with the following lines of code:

```
Template.home.helpers({
  postsList: function(){
    return Posts.find({}, {sort: {timeCreated: -1}});
  }
});
```

As we can see, we returned the collections cursor directly in the helper. This return value then gets passed to the {{#each}} block helper in our `home` template, which will then iterate over each post while rendering the `postInList` template.

 Note that `Posts.find()` returns a cursor, which is more efficient when used in an {{#each}} block helper, whereas `Posts.find().fetch()` will return an array with the document objects. Using `fetch()`, we can manipulate the documents before returning them.

We pass an options object as the second parameter to the `find()` function. The option we are passing will sort the result based on `timeCreated` and -1. The -1 value means it will be sorted in descending order (1 means ascending order).

Now, when we check out our browser, we will see that all of our five posts are listed, as shown in the following screenshot:

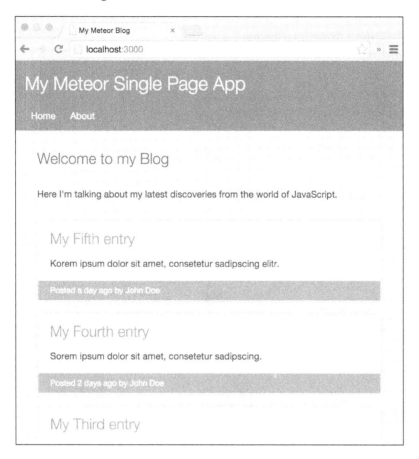

Updating a collection

Now that we know how to insert and fetch data, let's take a look at how to update data in our database.

As we've already seen before, we can use the console of our browser to play with the database. For our next examples, we will use only the console to see how Meteor reactively changes the templates when we change data.

To be able to edit a post in our database, we first need to know the `_id` field of its entry. To find this out, we need to type the following command:

```
Posts.find().fetch();
```

This will return us all the documents in the `Posts` collection, as we are not passing any specific query object.

In the returned array, we need to take a look at the last item, with the **My Fifth entry** title, and copy the `_id` field to the clipboard using *Cmd + C* (or *Ctrl + C* if we're on Windows or Linux).

> We can also simply use `Posts.findOne()`, which will give us the first document it finds.

Now that we have `_id`, we can simply update the title of our fifth post by typing the following command:

```
Posts.update('theCopied_Id', {$set: {title: 'Wow the title changed!'}});
```

As soon as we execute this command, we will notice that the title of the fifth post has changed to our new title, and if we now reload the page we will see that the title stays the same. This means the change was persistently made to the database.

To see Meteor's reactivity across clients, open up another browser window and navigate to `http://localhost:3000`. When we now change our title again by executing the following command, we will see that all the clients get updated in real time:

```
Posts.update('theCopied_Id', {$set: {title: 'Changed the title again'}});
```

Database everywhere

In Meteor, we can use the browser console to update data, which means that we can update the database from the client. This works because Meteor automatically syncs these changes to the server and updates the database accordingly.

This happens because we have the `autopublish` and `insecure` core packages added to our project by default. The `autopublish` package automatically publishes all documents to every client, whereas the `insecure` package allows every client to update database records by its `_id` field. Obviously, this works well for prototyping but is infeasible for production, as every client can manipulate our database.

If we remove the `insecure` package, we will need to add "allow and deny" rules to determine what a client is allowed to update and what they are not; otherwise, all updates will get denied. We will take a look at setting these rules in a later chapter, but for now this package serves us well, as we can immediately manipulate the database.

In the next chapter, we will see how to manually publish only certain documents to a client. We will start that by removing the `autopublish` package.

Differences between client and server collections

Meteor has a *database everywhere* approach. This means it provides the same API on the client as well as on the server. The data flow is controlled using a publication subscription model.

On the server sits the real MongoDB database, which stores data persistently. On the client, Meteor has a package called `minimongo`, which is a pure in-memory database mimicking most of MongoDB's query and update functions.

Every time a client connects to its Meteor server, Meteor downloads the documents that the client has subscribed to and stores them in its local `minimongo` database. From here, they can be displayed in a template or processed by functions.

When the client updates a document, Meteor syncs it back to the server, where it is passed through any allow/deny functions before being persistently stored in the database. This also works the other way; when a document in the server-side database changes, it will automatically sync to every client that is subscribed to it, keeping every connected client up to date.

Summary

In this chapter, we learned how to store data persistently in Meteor's MongoDB database. We also saw how we can query collections and update documents. We understood what the "database everywhere" approach means and how Meteor keeps every client up to date.

To dig deeper into MongoDB and to query and update collections, take a look at the following resources:

* https://www.meteor.com/full-stack-db-drivers
* https://www.meteor.com/mini-databases
* https://docs.meteor.com/#/full/collections
* http://docs.mongodb.org/manual/core/crud-introduction/
* http://docs.mongodb.org/manual/reference/operator/query/

You can find this chapter's code examples either at `https://www.packtpub.com/books/content/support/17713` or on GitHub at `https://github.com/frozeman/book-building-single-page-web-apps-with-meteor/tree/chapter3`.

In the next chapter, we will see how to control the data flow using publications and subscriptions so that we send only the necessary documents to the clients.

4
Controlling the Data Flow

In the previous chapter, we learned how to store data in our database persistently. In this chapter, we will take a look at how we can tell Meteor what to send to the clients.

Until now, this all worked magically because we used the `autopublish` package, which synced all of the data with every client. Now, we will control this flow manually, sending only the necessary data to the client.

In this chapter, we'll cover the following topics:

- Synchronizing data with the server
- Publishing data to clients
- Publishing partial collections
- Publishing only the specific fields of documents
- Lazy loading more posts

If you want to jump right into the chapter and follow the examples, download the previous chapter's code examples from either the book's web page at `https://www.packtpub.com/books/content/support/17713`, or from the GitHub repository at `https://github.com/frozeman/book-building-single-page-web-apps-with-meteor/tree/chapter3`.

These code examples will also contain all the style files, so we don't have to worry about adding CSS code along the way.

Syncing data – the current Web versus the new Web

In the current Web, most pages are either static files hosted on a server or dynamically generated by a server on a request. This is true for most server-side-rendered websites, for example, those written with PHP, Rails, or Django. Both of these techniques required no effort besides being displayed by the clients; therefore, they are called *thin* clients.

In modern web applications, the idea of the browser has moved from thin clients to *fat* clients. This means most of the website's logic resides on the client and the client asks for the data it needs.

Currently, this is mostly done via calls to an API server. This API server then returns data, commonly in JSON form, giving the client an easy way to handle it and use it appropriately.

Most modern websites are a mixture of thin and fat clients. Normal pages are server-side-rendered, where only some functionality, such as a chat box or news feed, is updated using API calls.

Meteor, however, is built on the idea that it's better to use the calculation power of all clients instead of one single server. A pure fat client or a single-page app contains the entire logic of a website's frontend, which is send down on the initial page load.

The server then merely acts as a data source, sending only the data to the clients. This can happen by connecting to an API and utilizing AJAX calls, or as with Meteor, using a model called **publication/subscription**. In this model, the server offers a range of publications and each client decides which dataset it wants to subscribe to.

Compared with AJAX calls, the developer doesn't have to take care of any downloading or uploading logic. The Meteor client syncs all of the data automatically in the background as soon as it subscribes to a specific dataset. When data on the server changes, the server sends the updated documents to the clients and vice versa, as shown in the following diagram:

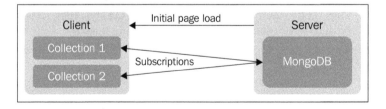

If this does sound insecure, be assured that we can set rules that filter changes on the server side. We will take a look at these possibilities in *Chapter 8, Security with the Allow and Deny Rules.*

Removing the autopublish package

To work with Meteor's publications/subscriptions, we need to remove the `autopublish` package, which was added by default to our project.

This package is useful for rapid prototyping, but infeasible in production since all of the data in our database would be synced to all the clients. This is not only insecure but also slows down the data loading process.

We just run the following command from inside our `my-meteor-blog` folder on the terminal:

```
$ meteor remove autopublish
```

Now we can run `meteor` again to start our server. When we check out the website, we will see that all our posts from the previous chapter are gone.

They are not really gone, however. The current server just didn't publish any yet, and the client just didn't subscribe to any; therefore, we can't see them.

Publishing data

In order to access the post on the client again, we need to tell the server to publish it to subscribing clients.

To do so, we will create a file called `publications.js` inside the `my-meteor-blog/server` folder and add the following lines of code:

```
Meteor.publish('all-posts', function () {
  return Posts.find();
});
```

The `Meteor.publish` function will create a publication called `all-posts` and return a cursor with all the posts from the `Post` collection in that publication.

Now, we only have to tell the client to subscribe to this publication and we will see our posts again.

We create a file called `subscriptions.js` inside the `my-meteor-blog/client` folder with the following content:

```
Meteor.subscribe('all-posts');
```

Now, when we check out our website, we can see that our blog posts have reappeared.

This happens because the client will subscribe to the `all-posts` publication when the `subsciptions.js` file is executed, which happens right before the page is fully loaded, as Meteor adds the `subsciptions.js` file automatically to the head of the document for us.

This means that the Meteor server sends the website first and the JavaScript builds the HTML on the client; then, all the subscriptions get synced, which populate the client's collections, and the template engine, **Blaze**, can display the posts.

Now that we have our posts back, let's see how we can tell Meteor to send only a subset of the documents from the collection.

Publishing only parts of data

To make our front page future-ready, we will need to limit the amount of posts shown on it, as we will probably have a lot of posts added with time.

For this, we will create a new publication called `limited-posts`, where we can pass a `limit` option to the posts' `find()` function and add it to our `publications.js` file, as follows:

```
Meteor.publish('limited-posts', function () {
  return Posts.find({}, {
    limit: 2,
    sort: {timeCreated: -1}
  });
});
```

We add a `sort` option, with which we sort the posts in descending order on the `timeCreated` field. This is necessary to ensure that we get the latest posts and then limit the output. If we only sort the data on the client, it might happen that we leave out newer posts, as the server publication would send only the first two documents it found, regardless of whether they are the latest ones or not.

Now we just have to go to `subscriptions.js` and change the subscription to the following line of code:

```
Meteor.subscribe('limited-posts');
```

If we check out our browser now, we will see that only the last two posts appear on our front page, since we only subscribed to two, as shown in the following screenshot:

We must be aware that if we keep the code for the old subscription alongside the code for the new subscription, we will subscribe to both. This means Meteor merges both subscriptions and therefore keeps all the subscribed documents in our client-side collections.

We need to either comment out the old subscription or remove it before adding the new one.

Publishing specific fields

To improve publications, we can also determine which fields we want to publish from the document. For example, we can only ask for the `title` and `text` properties instead of all other properties.

This speeds up the synchronization of our subscriptions since we don't require the whole post but only the necessary data and short descriptions when listing posts on the front page.

Let's add another publication to our `publications.js` file:

```
Meteor.publish('specificfields-posts', function () {
  return Posts.find({}, {
    fields: {
      title: 1
    }
  });
});
```

As this is just an example, we pass an empty object as a query to find all the documents, and as the second parameter to `find()`, we pass an options object containing the `fields` object.

Every field that we give a value of `1` will be included in the returned document. If we rather want to work by excluding fields, we can use the field name and set the value to `0`. However, we can't use both including and excluding fields, so we need to choose what fits better, depending on the document size.

Now we can simply change the subscription in our `subscriptions.js` file to the following line of code:

```
Meteor.subscribe('specificfields-posts');
```

Now, when we open the browser, it will present us with a list of our posts. Only the titles are present and the description, time, and author fields are empty:

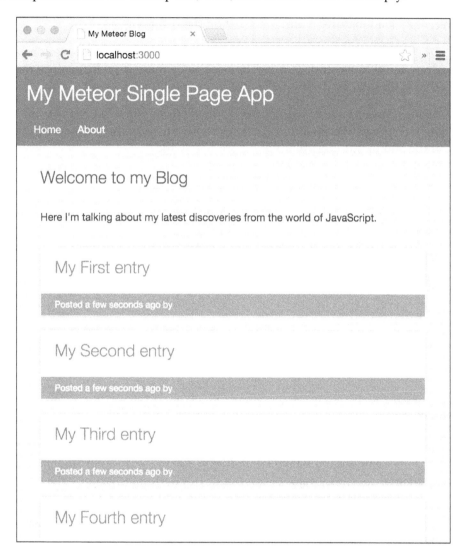

Lazy loading posts

Now that we've gone through these simple examples, let's put them all together and add a nice lazy load feature to our posts' list on the front page.

Lazy loading is a technique that loads additional data only when the user desires it or when they scroll to the end. This can be used to increase page load, since the data to be loaded is limited. To do this, let's perform the following steps:

1. We need to add a lazy load button to the bottom of the list of posts on the front page. We go to our `home.html` file and add the following button at the end of our `home` template, right below the `{{#each postsList}}` block helper:

   ```
   <button class="lazyload">Load more</button>
   ```

2. Next, we will add the publication that will send a flexible number of posts to our `publications.js` file, as follows:

   ```
   Meteor.publish('lazyload-posts', function (limit) {
     return Posts.find({}, {
       limit: limit,
       fields: {
         text: 0
       },
       sort: {timeCreated: -1}
     });
   });
   ```

Basically, it's a combination of what we learned earlier.

- We used the `limit` option, but instead of setting a fixed number, we used the `limit` parameter, which we will later pass to this publication function.

- Previously, we used the `fields` option and excluded the `text` field.

- We can just include `fields` to get the same result. This will be safer, as it ensures that we won't get any extra fields in case the documents get extended:

  ```
  fields: {
    title: 1,
    slug: 1,
    timeCreated: 1,
    description: 1,
    author: 1
  }
  ```

- We sorted the output to make sure we are always returning the latest posts.

Now that we have set our publication, let's add a subscription so that we can receive its data.

 Be aware that we need to remove any other subscription beforehand so that we are not subscribing to any other publication.

To do this, we need to make use of Meteor's `session` object. This object can be used on the client side to set variables reactively. This means every time we change this session's variable, it will run every function that uses it again. In the following example, we will use the session to increase our posts' lists' number when clicking on the lazy load button:

1. First, in the `subscription.js` file, we add the following lines of code:

```
Session.setDefault('lazyloadLimit', 2);
Tracker.autorun(function(){
Meteor.subscribe('lazyload-posts', Session.get('lazyloadLimit'));
});
```

2. Then we set the `lazyloadLimit` session variable to `2`, which will be the initial number of posts shown on the front page.

3. Next, we create a `Tracker.autorun()` function. This function will run at the start time and later at any time when we change the `lazyloadLimit` session variable to another value.

4. Inside this function, we subscribe to `lazyload-posts`, giving the `lazyloadLimit` value as a second parameter. This way, every time the session variable changes, we change our subscription with a new value.

5. Now we only need to increase the session value by clicking on the lazy load button and the subscription will change, sending us additional posts. To do this, we add the following lines of code to our `home.js` file at the end:

```
Template.home.events({
  'click button.lazyload': function(e, template){
  var currentLimit = Session.get('lazyloadLimit');

  Session.set('lazyloadLimit', currentLimit + 2);
  }
});
```

This code will attach a `click` event to the lazy load button. Every time we click on this button, we get the `lazyloadLimit` session and it increases by two.

6. When we check out our browser, we should be able to click on the lazy load button at the bottom of our posts list and it should add two more posts. This should happen every time we click on the button until we reach our five example posts.

This doesn't make much sense when we have only five posts, but when there are more than 50 posts, limiting the initially shown posts to 10 will noticeably speed up page loading time.

We then need to change only the session's default value to 10 and increase it by 10, and we have a nice lazy loading effect.

Switching subscriptions

Now that we have the nice logic of lazy loading in place, let's take a look at what happens here under the hood.

The `.autorun()` function , which we created earlier, will run the first time the code gets executed, subscribing us to the `lazyload-posts` publication. Meteor then sends the first two documents of the `Posts` collection, as the `limit` we first sent is 2.

The next time we change the `lazyloadLimit` session, it changes the subscription by changing the limit to the value we passed to the publication function.

Meteor then checks which documents exist in our client-side database in the background and requests to download the missing ones.

This will also work the other way when we decrease the session value. Meteor removes the documents that don't match the current subscription/subscriptions.

So, we can try this; we open the console of our browser and set the session limit to 5:

```
Session.set('lazyloadLimit', 5);
```

This will immediately display all five example posts in our list. When we now set it back to a smaller value, we will see how they are removed:

```
Session.set('lazyloadLimit', 2);
```

To ensure that they are gone, we can query our local database to check, as follows:

```
Posts.find().fetch();
```

This will return us an array of two items, showing that Meteor removed the posts that we are not subscribing to anymore, as shown in the following screenshot:

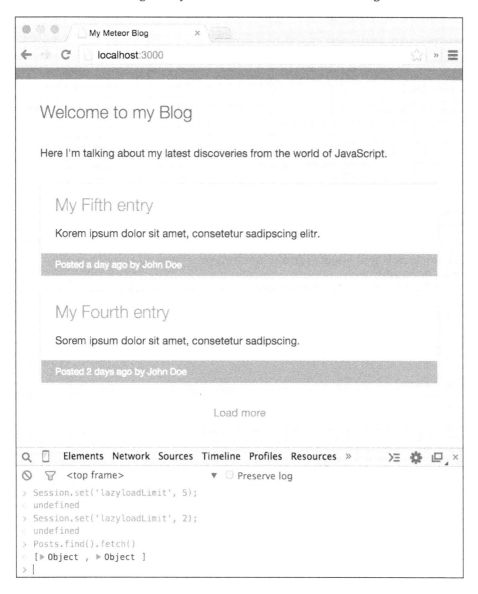

Some notes on data publishing

The publication and subscription model makes it fairly easy to receive and send data to the client, but as with every call to the server, sending and requesting data is expensive, as the server and the client both have to process the requests. Therefore, keep a few things in mind when building an app:

- Subscribe only to the documents that are necessary to make up the screen.

- Avoid sending fields with large content when we don't need them. This keeps our data stream leaner and faster.

- If we're using `limit` or `skip` in our publication, we need to make sure we're sorting it on the server so that we get the required data first and not some wrong tail of it.

You also should be aware that the `Meteor.publish()` function is not reactive. This means you can't use make one cursor depending on the result of another one, like you would mostly do on the client. For example, the following code snippet will not work, as it will never rerun when the comment count in the `Posts` collection changes:

```
Meteor.publish('comments', function (postId) {
    var post = Posts.find({_id: postId});

    return Comments.find({_id: {$in: post.comments}});
});
```

To solve this, you can either publish posts and comments separately and connect them in the client or use a third-party package, which allows for reactive publications such as the great `reywood:publish-composite` package at `https://atmospherejs.com/reywood/publish-composite`.

 Note that the only case where the `Meteor.publish()` function reruns is when the *current user* changes so that `this.userId` which is accessible in this function will change.

Summary

In this chapter, we created a few publications and subscribed to them. We used the `fields` and `limit` options to modify the number of published documents and created a simple lazy load logic for the front page of our blog.

To dig deeper into what we learned, we can take a look at *Chapter 3*, *Storing Data and Handling Collections*. While the following Meteor documentation will give us details about the options we can use in the collections `find()` functions:

- `https://www.meteor.com/livequery`
- `https://www.meteor.com/ddp`
- `https://docs.meteor.com/#/full/publishandsubscribe`
- `https://docs.meteor.com/#/full/collections`

You can find this chapter's code examples at `https://www.packtpub.com/books/content/support/17713` or on GitHub at `https://github.com/frozeman/book-building-single-page-web-apps-with-meteor/tree/chapter4`.

In the next chapter, we will give our app what makes a real app — different pages and routes.

5
Making Our App Versatile with Routing

Since we've made it to this chapter, we should already have a good understanding of Meteor's template system and how data synchronization between a server and clients works. After digesting this knowledge, let's get back to the fun part and make our blog a real website with different pages.

You might ask, "What do pages do in a single-page app?" The term "single page" is a bit confusing, as it doesn't mean that our app consists of only one page. It's rather a term derived from the current way of doing things, as there is only one page sent down from the server. After that, all the routing and paging happens in the browser. There aren't any pages requested from the server itself anymore. A better term here would be "client-side web application," though **single page** is the current used name.

In this chapter, we will cover the following topics:

- Writing routes for our static and dynamic pages
- Changing subscriptions based on routes
- Changing the title of the website for each page

So let's not waste time and get started by adding the `iron:router` package.

If you've jumped right into the chapter and want to follow the examples, download the previous chapter's code examples from either the book's web page at `https://www.packtpub.com/books/content/support/17713` or from the GitHub repository at `https://github.com/frozeman/book-building-single-page-web-apps-with-meteor/tree/chapter4`.

These code examples will also contain all the style files, so we don't have to worry about adding CSS code along the way.

Adding the iron:router package

Routes are the URLs of a specific page in our app. In a server-side-rendered app, routes are defined either by the server's/framework's configuration or the folder structure on the server.

In a client-side app, routes are simply paths that the app will use to determine which pages to render.

The steps to perform inside the client are as follows:

1. The website is sent down to the client.
2. The JavaScript file (or files) is loaded and parsed.
3. The router code will check which current URL it is on and run the correct route function, which will then render the right templates.

 To use routes in our app, we will make use of the `iron:router` package, a router specifically written for Meteor, which makes it easy to set up routes and combine them with subscriptions.

4. To add the package, we cancel any running Meteor instance, go to our `my-meteor-blog` folder, and type the following command:

   ```
   $ meteor add iron:router
   ```

5. If we are done with this, we can start Meteor again by running the `$ meteor` command.

When we go back to the console of our browser, we will see an error saying: `Error: Oh no! No route found for path: "/"`. Don't worry; we will deal with this in the next section.

Setting up the router

In order to use the router, we need to set it up. To keep our code organized, we will create a file called `routes.js` directly in the root of our `my-meteor-blog` folder with the following code:

```
Router.configure({
    layoutTemplate: 'layout'
});
```

The router configuration allows you to define the following default templates:

layoutTemplate	The layout template will be used as the main wrapper. Here, subtemplates will be rendered in the {{> yield}} placeholder, which has to be placed somewhere in the template.
notFoundTemplate	This template will be rendered if the current URL has no defined route.
loadingTemplate	This template will be shown when subscriptions for the current route are loading.

For our blog, we will just define the layoutTemplate property for now.

Perform the following steps to set up the router:

1. To create our first route, we need to add the following lines of code to the route.js file:

```
Router.map(function() {

    this.route('Home', {
        path: '/',
        template: 'home'
    });

});
```

> You can also name the Home route as home (in lowercase). Then we can leave the manual template definition out, as iron:router will look automatically for a template called home for that route.
>
> For simplicity, we define the template manually to keep all routes consistent throughout the book.

2. If we now save this file and get back to our browser, we will see the layout template rendered twice. This happens not because iron:router adds layoutTemplate by default to the body of our app, but because we added it manually as well as by using {{> layout}} in index.html, it gets rendered twice.

To prevent the double appearance of the layout template, we need to remove the {{> layout}} helper from the <body> tag inside our index.html file.

When we check out the browser, we will now see the layout template rendered only once.

Switching to a layout template

Even though we passed a template to our Home route using `template: home`, we are not rendering this template dynamically; we are just showing the layout template with its *hardcoded* subtemplates.

To change this, we need to replace the `{{> home}}` inclusion helper inside our layout template with `{{> yield}}`.

The `{{> yield}}` helper is a placeholder helper provided by `iron:router`, where route templates get rendered.

After doing this, when we check out the browser, we shouldn't see any change, as we are still rendering the `home` template, but this time dynamically. Then we proceed as follows:

1. In order to see whether this is true, we will add a not found template to our app, by adding the following template to our `layout.html` file after the layout template:

    ```
    <template name="notFound">
      <div class="center">
        <h1>Nothing here</h1><br>
        <h2>You hit a page which doesn't exist!</h2>
      </div>
    </template>
    ```

2. Now we need to add the `notFoundTemplate` property to the `Router.configure()` function of `route.js`:

    ```
    Router.configure({
        layoutTemplate: 'layout',
        notFoundTemplate: 'notFound'
    });
    ```

When we now navigate to `http://localhost:3000/doesntexist` in our browser, we will see the `notFound` template being rendered instead of our `home` template:

If we click on the **Home** link in the main menu, we will get back to our front page, as this link was navigating to "/". We have successfully added our first route. Now let's move on to create the second route.

Adding another route

Having a front page doesn't make a real website. Let's add a link to our **About** page, which has been in our drawer since *Chapter 2, Building HTML Templates*.

To do this, just duplicate the Home route and change the values to create an About route, as follows:

```
Router.map(function() {

    this.route('Home', {
        path: '/',
        template: 'home'
    });
```

```
        this.route('About', {
            path: '/about',
            template: 'about'
        });
    });
```

That's it!

Now, when we go back to our browser, we can click on the two links in the main menu to switch between our **Home** and **About** pages, and even typing in `http://localhost:3000/about` will bring us straight to the corresponding page, as shown in the following screenshot:

Moving the posts subscription to the Home route

In order to load the right data for each page, we need to have the subscription in the routes instead of keeping it in the separate `subscriptions.js` file.

The `iron:router` has a special function called `subscriptions()`, which is ideal for that purpose. Using this function, we can reactively update subscriptions belonging to a specific route.

To see it in action, add the `subscriptions()` function to our Home route:

```
this.route('Home', {
    path: '/',
    template: 'home',
    subscriptions: function(){
        return Meteor.subscribe("lazyload-posts", Session.
get('lazyloadLimit'));
    }
});
```

The **Session.setDefault('lazyloadLimit', 2)** line from the
subscriptions.js file needs to be placed at the start of the `routes.js`
file and before the `Router.configure()` function:

```
if(Meteor.isClient) {
    Session.setDefault('lazyloadLimit', 2);
}
```

This has to wrapped inside the `if(Meteor.isClient){}` condition, as the session
object is only available on the client.

The `subscriptions()` function is *reactive* like the `Tracker.autorun()` function
we used before. This means it will rerun and change the subscription when the
`lazyloadLimit` session variable changes.

In order to see it working, we need to delete the `my-meteor-blog/client/`
`subscriptions.js` file, so there are not two points where we subscribe to the
same publication.

When we now check the browser and refresh the page, we will see the home template
still shows all the example posts. Clicking on the lazy-load button increases the
number of posts listed, though this time everything happens through our reactive
`subscriptions()` function.

 The `iron:router` comes with more hooks, which you
can find as a short list in the *Appendix*.

To complete our routes, we only need to add the post routes, so we can click on a
post and read it in full detail.

Setting up the post route

To be able to show a full post page, we need to create a post template, which can be loaded when the user clicks on a post.

We create a file called `post.html` inside our `my-meteor-blog/client/templates` folder with the following template code:

```
<template name="post">
  <h1>{{title}}</h1>
  <h2>{{description}}</h2>

  <small>
    Posted {{formatTime timeCreated "fromNow"}} by {{author}}
  </small>

  <div class="postContent">
    {{#markdown}}
{{text}}
    {{/markdown}}
  </div>
</template>
```

This simple template displays all the information of a blog post and even reuses our `{{formatTime}}` helper we created earlier in this book from our `template-helper.js` file. We used this to format at the time the post was created.

We can't see this template yet, as we first have to create a publication and route for this page.

Creating a single-post publication

In order to show the full post's data in this template, we need to create another publication that will send the complete post document to the client.

To do so, we open our `my-meteor-blog/server/publication.js` file and add the following publication:

```
Meteor.publish("single-post", function(slug) {
  return Posts.find({slug: slug});
});
```

The `slug` parameter, which has been used here, will be later provided from our subscription method so that we can use the `slug` parameter to reference the correct post.

> A slug is a document title, which is formatted in a way that is usable in a URL. Slugs are better than just appending the document ID to the URL, as they are readable and understandable by visitors. They are also an important part of a good SEO.
>
> So that we can use slugs, every slug has to be unique. We will take care of that when we create the posts.

Assuming that we pass the right slug such as `my-first-entry`, this publication will send down the post containing this slug.

Adding the post route

In order for this route to work, it needs to be dynamic because every linked URL has to be different for each post.

We will also render a loading template until the post is loaded. To start, we add the following template to our `my-meteor-blog/client/templates/layout.html`:

```
<template name="loading">
  <div class="center">
    <h1>Loading</h1>
  </div>
</template>
```

Additionally, we have to add this template as the default loading template to our `Router.configure()` call in the `routes.js`:

```
Router.configure({
    layoutTemplate: 'layout',
    notFoundTemplate: 'notFound',
    loadingTemplate: 'loading',
    ...
```

We then add the following lines of code to our `Router.map()` function to create a dynamic route:

```
this.route('Post', {
    path: '/posts/:slug',
    template: 'post',

    waitOn: function() {
        return Meteor.subscribe('single-post', this.params.slug);
    },
```

```
        data: function() {
            return Posts.findOne({slug: this.params.slug});
        }
    });
```

The `'/posts/:slug'` path is a dynamic route, where `:slug` can be anything and will be passed to the routes functions as `this.params.slug`. This way we can simply pass the given slug to the `single-post` subscription and retrieve the correct document for the post matching this slug.

The `waitOn()` function works like the `subscriptions()` function, though will automatically render `loadingTemplate`, we set in the `Router.configure()` until the subscriptions are ready.

The `data()` function in this route will set the data context of the `post` template. We basically look in our local database for a post containing the given slug from the URL.

 The `findOne()` method of the `Posts` collection works like `find()`, but returns only the first found result as a JavaScript object.

Let's sum up what happens here:

1. The route gets called (through a clicked link or by reloading of the page).
2. The `waitOn()` function will then subscribe to the right post identified by the given `slug` parameter, which is a part of the URL.
3. Because of the `waitOn()` function, the `loadingTemplate` will be rendered until the subscription is ready. Since this will happen very fast on our local machine, so we probably won't see the loading template at all.
4. As soon as the subscription is synced, the template gets rendered.
5. The `data()` function will then rerun, setting the data context of the template to the current post document.

Now that the publication and the route are ready, we can simply navigate to `http://localhost:3000/posts/my-first-entry` and we should see the `post` template appear.

Linking the posts

Although we've set up the route and subscription, we can't see it work, as we need the right links to the posts. As each of our previously added example posts already contains a `slug` property, we just have to add them to the links to our posts in the `postInList` template. Open the `my-meteor-blog/client/templates/postInList.html` file and change the link as follows:

```
<h2><a href="posts/{{slug}}">{{title}}</a></h2>
```

Finally, when we go to our browser and click on the title of a blog post, we get redirected to a page that shows the full post entry, like the entry shown in the following screenshot:

Changing the website's title

Now that we have the routes of our posts working, we are only missing the right titles being displayed for each page.

Sadly, <head></head> is not a reactive template in Meteor, where we could let Meteor do the work of changing titles and meta tags.

> It is planned to make the head tag a reactive template, but probably not before version 1.0.

To change the document title, we need to come up with a different way of changing it, based on the current route.

Luckily, iron:router has the onAfterAction() function, which can also be used in the Router.configure() function to run before every route. In this function, we have access to the data context of the current route, so we can simply set the title using native JavaScript:

```
Router.configure({
    layoutTemplate: 'layout',
    notFoundTemplate: 'notFound',

    onAfterAction: function() {
        var data = Posts.findOne({slug: this.params.slug});

        if(_.isObject(data) && !_.isArray(data))
            document.title = 'My Meteor Blog - '+ data.title;
        else
            document.title = 'My Meteor Blog - '+ this.route.
getName();
    }
});
```

Using **Posts.findOne({slug: this.params.slug})**, we get the current post of the route. We then check whether it's an object; if so, we add the post title to the title metatag. Otherwise, we just take the route name.

Doing this in Router.configure() will call the **onAfterAction** for every route.

If we now take a look at our browser's tab, we will see that the title of our website changes when we move throughout the website:

 If we want to make our blog cooler, we can add the `mrt:iron-router-progress` package. This will add a progress bar at the top of our pages when changing routes. We just need to run the following command from our app's folder:

```
$ meteor add mrt:iron-router-progress
```

Summary

That's it! Our app is now a fully working website with different pages and URLs.

In this chapter, we learned how to set up static and dynamic routes. We moved our subscriptions to the routes so that they change automatically, based on the route's needs. We also used slugs to subscribe to the right posts and displayed them in the `post` template. Finally, we changed our website's title so that it matches the current route.

To learn more about `iron:router`, take a look at its documentation at `https://github.com/EventedMind/iron-router`.

You can find this chapter's code examples either at `https://www.packtpub.com/books/content/support/17713` or on GitHub at `https://github.com/frozeman/book-building-single-page-web-apps-with-meteor/tree/chapter5`.

In the next chapter, we will take a deeper look at Meteor's session object.

6

Keeping States with Sessions

We already used Meteor's session object when we implemented our lazy load technique in an earlier chapter. In this chapter, we want to take a deeper look at it and learn how it can be used to create template-specific reactive functions.

In this chapter, we will cover the following topics:

- What sessions are
- How hot code pushes affect sessions
- Rerunning template helpers using sessions
- Rerunning functions
- Creating template-specific reactive functions

> If you've jumped right into the chapter and want to follow the examples, download the previous chapter's code examples from either the book's web page at `https://www.packtpub.com/books/content/support/17713` or from the GitHub repository at `https://github.com/frozeman/book-building-single-page-web-apps-with-meteor/tree/chapter5`.
>
> These code examples will also contain all the style files, so we don't have to worry about adding CSS code along the way.

Meteor's session object

The `Session` object provided by Meteor is a reactive data source and serves mainly to preserve global states throughout hot code reloads, though it won't preserve its data when the page is manually reloaded, making it different from PHP sessions.

A hot code reload happens when we upload new code and the server pushes those updates to all clients.

The `Session` object is a reactive data source. This means wherever this session variable is used in a reactive function, it will rerun that function when its value changes.

One use of the session variable can be to maintain global states of our app, for example, to check whether the user has their sidebar visible or not.

The session object is not useful for simple data communication between templates and other parts of the app, as maintaining this would quickly become a nightmare and naming collisions could occur.

A better way for simple reactivity

If we wanted to use something for intra-app communication, it's better to use Meteors `reactive-var` package, which comes with a `Session` like `ReactiveVar` object.

To use it, we can simply add it using `$ meteor add reactive-var`.

This object then needs to be instantiated and comes with a reactive `get()` and `set()` function like the `session` object:

```
Var myReactiveVar = new ReactiveVar('my initial value');

// now we can get it in any reactive function
myReactiveVar.get();

// and set it, to rerun depending functions
myReactiveVar.set('my new value');
```

For more custom reactivity, we can build our own custom reactive object using Meteor's `Tracker` package. To read more about this, refer to Chapter 9, *Advanced Reactivity*.

 For reactive variables that are tied to a specific template instance, check out my `frozeman:template-var` package at `https://atmospherejs.com/frozeman/template-var`.

Using sessions in template helpers

As all template helper functions are reactive functions, a good place to use a session object is inside such a helper.

Reactive means that when we use a reactive object inside this function, that function will rerun when the reactive object changes, additionally rerendering this part of the template.

 Template helpers are not the only reactive functions; we can also create our own using `Tracker.autorun(function(){...})`, as we saw in earlier chapters.

To demonstrate the usage of sessions in a template helper, perform the following steps:

1. Let's open our `my-meteor-blog/client/templates/home.js` file and add the following helper code anywhere in the file:

```
Template.home.helpers({
  //...
  sessionExample: function(){
    return Session.get('mySessionExample');
  }
});
```

   This creates the `sessionExample` helper, which returns the value of the `mySessionExample` session variable.

2. Next, we need to add this helper to our `home` template itself by opening the `my-metepr-blog/client/templates/home.html` file and adding the helper above our `{{#each postsList}}` block helper:

```
<h2>This comes from our Session: <strong>{{sessionExample}}</
strong></h2>
```

3. Now, let's open up our browser at `http://localhost:3000`. We will see the static text we add appearing in our blog's home page. Yet, to see Meteor's reactive session at work, we need to open up the browser's console and type the following line of code:

```
Session.set('mySessionExample', 'I just set this.');
```

This is illustrated in the following screenshot:

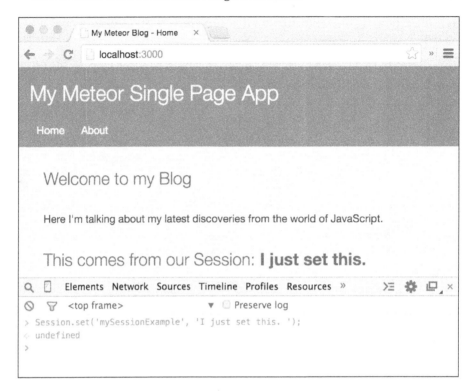

Immediately after we pressed *Enter*, we saw the text added to our template. This is because when we call `Session.set('mySessionExample', ...)`, Meteor will rerun every reactive function wherein we called `Session.get('mySessionExample')` before. For template helpers, this will rerun only this specific template helper, rerendering only this part of the template.

We can try this by setting different values for the `mySessionExample` session variable so that we can see how the text will change at all times.

Session and hot code pushes

A hot code push is when we change files and the Meteor server pushes these changes to the clients. Meteor is smart enough to reload the page, without losing the values of HTML forms or sessions. Therefore, sessions can be used to keep user states consistent over hot code pushes.

In order to see this, we set the value of `mySessionExample` to anything we want and see the website updating to this value.

When we now go to our `home.html` file and make a minor change, for example, removing `<strong>` around the `{{sessionExample}}` helper and saving the file, we see that our sessions state is kept, even though the page reloads with the new changed template. This is demonstrated in the following screenshot:

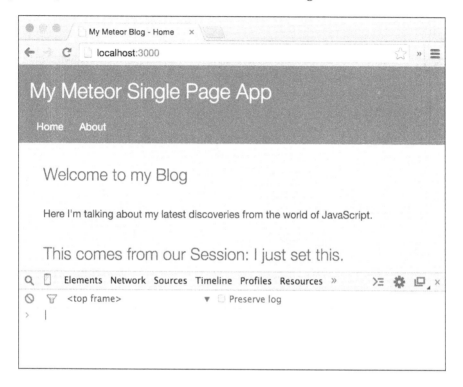

 If we manually reload the page using the browser's refresh button, the session will not be able to persist the change and the text will disappear.

To overcome this limitation, there are many packages in Meteor's package repository that reactively store data in the browser's local storage to persist across page reloads. One of them is called `persistent-session` and can be found at `http://atmospherejs.com/package/persistent-session`.

Rerunning functions reactively

To rerun functions based on session changes, Meteor provides the `Tracker.autorun()` function, which we used before to change the lazy load subscription.

The `Tracker.autorun()` function will make every function we pass to it reactive. To see a simple example, we will create a function that will alert a text every time the function reruns.

 The `Tracker` package is what the session uses under the hood to make the reactivity work. In *Chapter 9, Advanced Reactivity*, we will take a deeper look at this package.

Perform the following steps to rerun functions reactively:

1. Let's create a new file called `main.js`, but this time in the root of the `my-meteor-blog` folder, with the following content:

```
if(Meteor.isClient) {

    Tracker.autorun(function(){
        var example = Session.get('mySessionExample');
        alert(example);
    });
}
```

 We will need the `main.js` file in later chapters. Therefore, we created it in the root folder, making it accessible on the client and the server.

However, as Meteor's session object is only available on the client, we will use the `if(Meteor.isClient)` condition in order to execute the code only on the client.

When we now check out our browser, we will see an alert that displays `undefined`. This is because the function passed to `Tracker.autorun()` will also run when the code is executed, at a time when we haven't set our session.

2. To set a session variable's default value, we can use `Session.setDefault('mySessionExample', 'My Text')`. This will set the session without running any reactive functions, when the value of the session is `undefined`. If the value of the session variable was already set, `setDefault` won't change the variables at all.

3. In our example, we probably don't want an alert window to appear when the page is loaded. To prevent this first run, we can use the `Tracker.Computation` object, which is passed as the first argument to our function and which provides us with a property called `firstRun`. This property will be set to `true` at the first run of the function. When we use this, we can prevent the display of the alert at the start:

```
Tracker.autorun(function(c){
    var example = Session.get('mySessionExample');

    if(!c.firstRun) {
        alert(example);
    }
});
```

4. Now let's go to the browser's console and set the session to any value to see the alert appear:

```
Session.set('mySessionExample','Hi there!');
```

The output of this code is demonstrated in the following screenshot:

 When we run the same command again, we will not see the alert window show up, as Meteor is smart enough to prevent reruns when the session's value doesn't change. If we set it to another value, the alert will appear again.

Stopping reactive functions

The `Tracker.Computation` object, passed as the first argument, also gives us a way to stop the function from being reactive at all. To try this, we will change the function so that it stops its reactivity when we pass the `stop` string to the session:

```
Tracker.autorun(function(c){
    var example = Session.get('mySessionExample');

    if(!c.firstRun) {
        if(Session.equals('mySessionExample', 'stop')) {
            alert('We stopped our reactive Function');
            c.stop();
        } else {
            alert(example);
        }
    }
});
```

Now, when we go to our browser's console and run `Session.set('mySessionExample', 'stop')`, the reactive function will stop being reactive. To test this, we can try to run `Session.set('mySessionExample', 'Another text')` and we will see that the alert window won't appear.

 If we make a code change and a hot code reload happens, the reactive function will become reactive again, as the code was executed again.

The preceding example also uses a function called `Session.equals()`. This function can compare two scalar values while preventing unnecessary recomputations, compared to using `Session.get('mySessionExample) === 'stop'`. Using `Session.equals()` would only rerun this function when the session variable changes *to* or *from* that value.

 In our example, however, this function doesn't make a difference, as we called `Session.get()` before as well.

Using autorun in a template

Although it could be useful to use `Tracker.autorun()` globally in our app in some cases, it can become quickly hard to maintain those global reactive functions as our app grows.

Therefore, it is good practice to bind reactive functions to the templates for which they perform actions.

Luckily, Meteor offers a special version of `Tracker.autorun()` that is tied to a template instance and stops automatically when the template gets destroyed.

To make use of this, we can start the reactive function in the `created()` or `rendered` callback. To start, let's comment out our previous example from the `main.js` file so that we won't get two alert windows.

Open our `home.js` file and add the following lines of code:

```
Template.home.created = function(){

    this.autorun(function(){
        alert(Session.get('mySessionExample'));
    });
};
```

This will create the reactive function when the home template is created. When we go to the browser's console and set the `mySessionExample` session to a new value, we will see the alert window appear, as shown in the following screenshot:

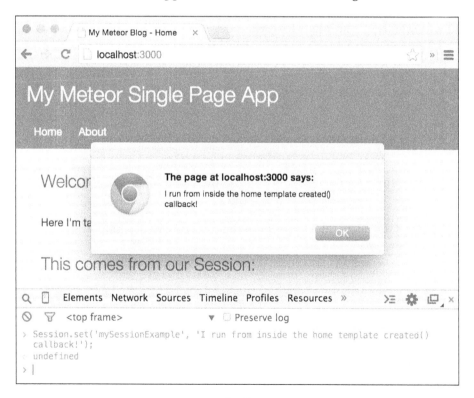

Now, when we switch the templates by clicking on the **About** link in the menu and we set the `mySessionExample` session variable again to another value using the browsers console, we won't see the alert window appear as the reactive `this.autorun()` was stopped when the template was destroyed.

> Note that all `Tracker.autorun()` functions return a `Tracker.Computation` object, which can be used to stop the reactivity of the autorun at any time using `Tracker.Computation.stop()`:
>
> ```
> Var myReactiveFunction = Tracker.autorun(function()
> {...});
> // Do something which needs to stop the autorun
> myReactiveFunction.stop();
> ```

The reactive session object

We've seen that the session object can rerun a function when its value is changed. This is the same behavior as that of the `find()` and `findOne()` functions of collections, which will rerun functions when the underlying data in the collection changes.

We can use sessions to keep user states across hot code pushes, such as states of drop-down menus or pop-ups. However, keep in mind that without a clear naming convention, these session variables can soon become hard to maintain.

For more specific reactive behavior, it is good to build a custom reactive object using Meteor's `Tracker` core package, which we will cover in *Chapter 9, Advanced Reactivity*.

Summary

In this chapter, we learned what we can do with Meteor's reactive session object. We used it to rerun template helpers and our own custom functions, and we made a reactive function template specific using the `created()` and `destroyed()` callbacks.

To dig deeper, take a look at Meteor's documentation about sessions and reactivity at the following resources:

- `https://docs.meteor.com/#/full/reactivity`
- `https://docs.meteor.com/#/full/session`
- `https://docs.meteor.com/#/full/reactivevar_pkg`
- `https://www.meteor.com/tracker`

You can find this chapter's code examples at `https://www.packtpub.com/books/content/support/17713` or on GitHub at `https://github.com/frozeman/book-building-single-page-web-apps-with-meteor/tree/chapter6`.

In the next chapter, we will create the admin user and backend for our blog, laying down the foundation to create and edit posts.

7
Users and Permissions

Having worked through the previous chapters, we should have a working blog by now. We can click on all links and posts, and even lazy load more posts.

In this chapter, we will add our backend login and create the admin user. We will also create the template to edit posts and make an edit button visible to the admin user so that they can edit and add new content.

In this chapter, we will learn the following concepts:

- Meteor's `accounts` package
- Creating users and a log in
- How to restrict certain routes to only logged-in users

You can delete all the session examples from the previous chapter, as we won't need them to progress with our app. Delete the session's code from `my-meteor-blog/main.js`, `my-meteor-blog/client/templates/home.js`, and `my-meteor-blog/client/templates/home.html`, or download a fresh copy of the previous chapter's code.

If you've jumped right into the chapter and want to follow the examples, download the previous chapter's code examples from either the book's web page at `https://www.packtpub.com/books/content/support/17713` or from the GitHub repository at `https://github.com/frozeman/book-building-single-page-web-apps-with-meteor/tree/chapter6`.

These code examples will also contain all the style files, so we don't have to worry about adding CSS code along the way.

Meteor's accounts packages

Meteor makes it very easy to add authentication to our web app using its `accounts` package. The `accounts` package is a complete login solution tied to Meteor's core. Created users can be identified by ID in many of Meteor's server-side functions, for example, in a publication:

```
Meteor.publish("examplePublication", function () {
    // the current loggedin user id can be accessed via
    this.userId;
}
```

Additionally, we can add support for login via Facebook, GitHub, Google, Twitter, Meetup, and Weibo by simply adding one or more of the `accounts-*` core packages.

Meteor also comes with a simple login interface, an extra template that can be added using the `{{> loginButtons}}` helper.

All registered user profiles will be stored in a collection called `Users`, which Meteor creates for us. All the processes in authentication and communication use the **Secure Remote Password (SRP)** protocol and most external services use OAuth.

For our blog, we will simply create one admin user, which when logged in will be able to create and edit posts.

If we want to use one of the third-party services to log in, we can work through this chapter first, and then add one of the previously mentioned packages.

After we add the additional packages, we can open up the **Sign in** form. We will see a button where we can configure the third-party services for use with our app.

Adding the accounts packages

To start using a login system, we need to add the `accounts-ui` and `accounts-password` packages to our app, as follows:

1. To do so, we open up the terminal, navigate to our `my-meteor-blog` folder, and type the following command:

    ```
    $ meteor add accounts-ui accounts-password
    ```

2. After we have successfully added the packages, we can run our app again using the `meteor` command.

3. As we want to prevent the creation of additional user accounts by our visitors, we need to disallow this functionality in our `accounts` package, `config`. First, we need to open up our `my-meteor-blog/main.js` file, which we created in the previous chapter, and remove all of the code, as we won't need the session examples anymore.

4. Then add the following lines of code to this file, but make sure you don't use `if(Meteor.isClient)`, as we want to execute the code on both the client and the server this time:

```
Accounts.config({
    forbidClientAccountCreation: true
});
```

This will forbid any call of `Accounts.createUser()` on the client and the `accounts-ui` package will not show the **Register** button to our visitors.

 This option doesn't seem to work for third-party services. So, when using third-party services, everybody can sign up and edit posts. To prevent this, we will need to create "deny" rules for user creation on the server side, which is beyond the scope of this chapter.

Adding admin functionality to our templates

The best way to allow editing of our post is to add an **Edit post** link to our post's page, which can only be seen if we are logged in. This way, we save rebuilding a similar infrastructure for an additional backend, and make it easy to use as there is no strong separation between frontend and backend.

First, we will add a **Create new post** link to our `home` template, then add the **Edit post** link to the post's `pages` template, and finally add the login buttons and form to the main menu.

Adding a link for new posts

Let's begin by adding a **Create new post** link. Open the `home` template at `my-meteor-blog/clients/templates/home.html` and add the following lines of code just above the `{{#each postsList}}` block helper:

```
{{#if currentUser}}
    <a href="/create-post" class="createNewPost">Create new post</a>
{{/if}}
```

The {{currentUser}} helper comes with the accounts-base package, which was installed when we installed our accounts packages. It will return the current logged-in user, or return null if no user is logged in. Using it inside an {{#if}} block helper allows us to show content only to logged-in users.

Adding the link to edit posts

To edit posts, we simply add an **Edit post** link to our post template. Open up post.html from the same folder and add {{#if currentUser}}..{{/if}} after {{author}}, as follows:

```
<small>
    Posted {{formatTime timeCreated "fromNow"}} by {{author}}

    {{#if currentUser}}
        | <a href="/edit-post/{{slug}}">Edit post</a>
    {{/if}}
</small>
```

Adding the login form

Now that we have both links to add and edit posts, let's add the login form. We can create our own form, but Meteor already comes with a simple login form, which we can style to fit our design.

Since we added the accounts-ui package previously, Meteor provides us with the {{> loginButtons}} template helper, which works as a drop-in-place template. To add this, we will open our layout.html template and add the following helper inside our menu's <ul></ul> tags, as follows:

```
<h1>My Meteor Single Page App</h1>
<ul>
    <li>
        <a href="/">Home</a>
    </li>
    <li>
        <a href="/about">About</a>
    </li>

</ul>

{{> loginButtons}}
```

Creating the template to edit posts

Now we are only missing the template to edit the posts. To add this, we will create a file called `editPost.html` inside our `my-meteor-blog/client/templates` folder, and fill it with the following lines of code:

```html
<template name="editPost">
  <div class="editPost">
    <form>
        <label>
          Title
          <input type="text" name="title" placeholder="Awesome title"
value="{{title}}">
        </label>

        <label>
          Description
          <textarea name="description" placeholder="Short description
displayed in posts list" rows="3">{{description}}</textarea>
        </label>

        <label>
          Content
          <textarea name="text" rows="10" placeholder="Brilliant
content">{{text}}</textarea>
        </label>

        <button type="submit" class="save">Save Post</button>
    </form>
  </div>
</template>
```

As we can see, we have added the helpers for `{{title}}`, `{{description}}`, and `{{text}}`, which will come later from the post's data. This simple template, with its three text fields, will allow us to edit and create new posts later.

If we now check out our browser, we will notice that we can't see any of the changes we made so far, apart from the **Sign in** link in the corner of our website. To be able to log in, we first need to add our admin user.

Creating the admin user

Since we deactivated the creation of users from the client, as a security measure we will create the admin user on the server in the same way we created our example posts.

Open the `my-meteor-blog/server/main.js` file and add the following lines of code somewhere inside `Meteor.startup(function(){...})`:

```
if(Meteor.users.find().count() === 0) {

    console.log('Created Admin user');

    Accounts.createUser({
        username: 'johndoe',
        email: 'johndoe@example.com',
        password: '1234',
        profile: {
            name: 'John Doe'
        }
    });
}
```

If we now go to our browser, we should be able to log in using the user we just created, and we immediately see that all the edit links appear.

However, when we click any of the edit links, we will see the `notFound` template appearing because we didn't create any of our admin routes yet.

Adding permissions

Meteor's `account` package doesn't come by default with configurable permissions for users.

To add permission control, we can add a third-party package such as the `deepwell:authorization` package, which can be found on Atmosphere at `http://atmospherejs.com/deepwell/authorization` and which comes with a complex role model.

If we want to do it manually, we can add the simple `roles` properties to our user document when we create the user, and then check for these roles in our allow/deny roles when we create or update posts. We will learn about allow/deny rules in the next chapter.

If we create a user using the `Accounts.createUser()` function, we can't add a custom property, so we need to update the user document after we have created the user, as follows:

```
var userId = Accounts.createUser({
  username: 'johndoe',
  email: 'johndoe@example.com',
  password: '1234',
  profile: {
    name: 'John Doe'
  }
});
// add the roles to our user
Meteor.users.update(userId, {$set: {
  roles: {admin: true},
}})
```

By default, Meteor publishes the `username`, `emails`, and `profile` properties of the currently logged-in user. To add additional properties, such as our custom `roles` property, we need to add a publication, to access the `roles` property on the client as well, as follows:

1. Open the `my-meteor/blog/server/publictions.js` file and add the following publication:

```
Meteor.publish("userRoles", function () {
  if (this.userId) {
   return Meteor.users.find({_id: this.userId}, {fields: {roles:
1}});
  } else {
   this.ready();
  }
});
```

2. In the `my-meteor-blog/main.js` file, we add the subscription as follows:

```
if(Meteor.isClient){
  Meteor.subscribe("userRoles");
}
```

3. Now that we have the `roles` property available on the client, we can change `{{#if currentUser}}..{{/if}}` in the `home` and `post` templates to `{{#if currentUser.roles.admin}}..{{/if}}` so that only admins can see the buttons.

A note on security

The user can only update their own `profile` property using the following command:

```
Meteor.users.update(ownUserId, {$set: {profiles:{myProperty: 'xyz'}}})
```

If we want to update the `roles` property, we will fail. To see this in action, we can open up the browser's console and type the following command:

```
Meteor.users.update(Meteor.user()._id, {$set:{ roles: {admin: false}}});
```

This will give us an error stating: **update failed: Access denied**, as shown in the following screenshot:

 If we want to allow users to edit other properties such as their `roles` property, we need to add a `Meteor.users.allow()` rule for that.

Creating routes for the admin

Now that we have an admin user, we can add the routes, which lead to the `editPost` template. Though in theory the `editPost` template is available to every client, it doesn't create any risk, as the allow and deny rules are the real security layer, which we will take a look at in the next chapter.

To add the route to create posts, let's open up our `my-meteor-blog/routes.js` file and add the following route to the `Router.map()` function:

```
this.route('Create Post', {
    path: '/create-post',
    template: 'editPost'
});
```

This will simply show the `editPost` template as soon as we click on the **Create new post** link on our home page, as shown in the following screenshot:

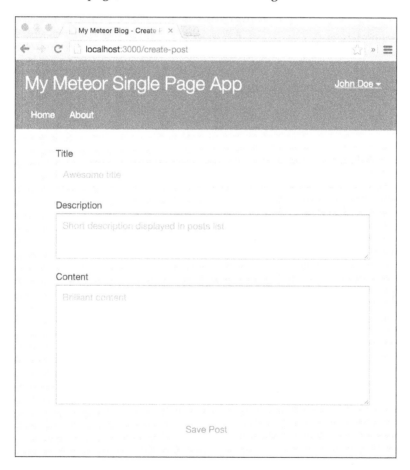

We see that the form is empty because we did not set any data context to the template, and therefore the {{title}}, {{description}}, and {{text}} placeholders in the template displayed nothing.

To make the edit post route work, we need to add subscriptions similar to those we did for the Post route itself. To keep things **DRY** (which means **Don't Repeat Yourself**), we can create a custom controller, which both routes will use, as follows:

1. Add the following lines of code after the Router.configure(...); call:

```
PostController = RouteController.extend({
    waitOn: function() {
        return Meteor.subscribe('single-post', this.params.slug);
    },

    data: function() {
        return Posts.findOne({slug: this.params.slug});
    }
});
```

2. Now we can simply edit the Post route, remove the waitOn() and data() functions, and add PostController instead:

```
this.route('Post', {
    path: '/posts/:slug',
    template: 'post',
    controller: 'PostController'
});
```

3. Now we can also add the Edit Post route by just changing the path and the template properties:

```
this.route('Edit Post', {
    path: '/edit-post/:slug',
    template: 'editPost',
    controller: 'PostController'
});
```

4. That's it! When we now go to our browser, we will be able to access any post and click on the **Edit** button, and we will be directed to editPost template.

If you are wondering why the form is filled in with the post data, take a look at PostController, which we just created. Here, we return the post document inside the data() function, setting the data context of the template to the post's data.

Now that we have these routes in place, we should be done. Shouldn't we?

Not yet, because everybody who knows the /create-post and /edit-post/my-title routes can simply see the editPost template, even if he or she is not an admin.

Preventing visitors from seeing the admin routes

To prevent visitors from seeing admin routes, we need to check whether the user is logged in before we show them the routes. The `iron:router` comes with a `Router.onBeforeAction()` hook, which can be run for all or some routes. We will use this to run a function to check whether the user is logged in; if not, we will pretend that the route doesn't exist and simply display the `notFound` template.

Add the following code snippet at the end of the `routes.js` file:

```
var requiresLogin = function(){
    if (!Meteor.user() ||
        !Meteor.user().roles ||
        !Meteor.user().roles.admin) {
        this.render('notFound');

    } else {
        this.next();
    }
};

Router.onBeforeAction(requiresLogin, {only: ['Create Post','Edit
Post']});
```

Here, first we create the `requiresLogin()` function, which will be executed before the `Create Post` and `Edit Post` routes because we pass them as the second arguments to the `Router.onBeforeAction()` function.

Inside the `requiresLogin()`, we check whether the user is logged in, which will return the user document when calling `Meteor.user()`, and if they have the role `admin`. If not, we simply render the `notFound` template and don't continue to the route. Otherwise, we run `this.next()`, which will continue to render the current route.

That's it! If we now log out and navigate to the `/create-post` route, we will see the `notfound` template.

If we log in, the template will switch and immediately show the `editPost` template.

This happens because the `requiresLogin()` function becomes reactive as soon as we pass it to `Router.onBeforeAction()`, and since `Meteor.user()` is a reactive object, any change to the user's status will rerun this function.

Now that we have created the admin user and the necessary templates, we can move on to actually creating and editing the posts.

Summary

In this chapter, we learned how to create and log in users, how we can show content and templates only to logged-in users, and how routes can be altered depending on the login status.

To learn more, take a look at the following links:

- `https://www.meteor.com/accounts`
- `https://docs.meteor.com/#/full/accounts_api`
- `https://docs.meteor.com/#/full/meteor_users`
- `http://en.wikipedia.org/wiki/Secure_Remote_Password_protocol`
- `https://github.com/EventedMind/iron-router/blob/devel/Guide.md#using-hooks`

You can find this chapter's code examples at `https://www.packtpub.com/books/content/support/17713` or on GitHub at `https://github.com/frozeman/book-building-single-page-web-apps-with-meteor/tree/chapter7`.

In the next chapter, we will learn how we can create and update posts and how to control updates to the database from the client side.

8
Security with the Allow and Deny Rules

In the previous chapter, we created our admin user and prepared the `editPost` template. In this chapter, we will make this template work so that we can create and edit posts using it.

To make it possible to insert and update documents in our database, we need to set constraints so that not everybody can change our database. In Meteor, this is done using the allow and deny rules. These functions will check documents before they are inserted into the database.

In this chapter, you will cover the following topics:

- Adding and updating posts
- Using the allow and deny rules to control the updating of the database
- Using methods on the server for more flexibility
- Using method stubs to enhance user experience

If you've jumped right into the chapter and want to follow the examples, download the previous chapter's code examples from either the book's web page at `https://www.packtpub.com/books/content/support/17713` or from the GitHub repository at `https://github.com/frozeman/book-building-single-page-web-apps-with-meteor/tree/chapter7`.

These code examples will also contain all the style files, so we don't have to worry about adding CSS code along the way.

Adding a function to generate slugs

In order to generate slugs from our post's titles, we will use the `underscore-string` library, which comes with a simple `slugify()` function. Luckily, a wrapper package for this library already exists on the Meteor package servers. To add it, we run the following command from the terminal in our `my-meteor-blog` folder:

```
$ meteor add wizonesolutions:underscore-string
```

This will extend `underscore`, which is used by default in Meteor, with extra string functions such as `_.slugify()`, to generate a slug from strings.

Creating a new post

Now that we can generate slugs for each created page, we can proceed to add the saving process to the `editPost` template.

To do so, we need to create a JavaScript file for our `editPost` template by saving a file called `editPost.js` to the `my-meteor-blog/client/templates` folder. Inside this file, we will add an event for the **Save** button of the template:

```
Template.editPost.events({
  'submit form': function(e, template){
    e.preventDefault();
    console.log('Post saved');
  }
});
```

Now, if we go to the `/create-post` route and click on the **Save Post** button, the **Post saved** log should appear in the browser's console.

Saving a post

In order to save the post, we will simply take the form's content and store it in the database. Later, we'll redirect to the newly created post page. To do so, we extend our click event with the following lines of code:

```
Template.editPost.events({
  'submit form': function(e, tmpl){
    e.preventDefault();
    var form = e.target,
        user = Meteor.user();
```

We get the current user so that we can add him later as the post's author. We then generate a slug from the post's title using our `slugify()` function:

```
var slug = _.slugify(form.title.value);
```

Following this, we insert the post document into the `Posts` collection using all other form fields. For the `timeCreated` property, we get the current Unix timestamp using the `moment` package, which we added in *Chapter 1, Getting Started with Meteor*.

The `owner` field will later help us to determine by which user this post was created:

```
Posts.insert({
            title:          form.title.value,
            slug:           slug,
            description:    form.description.value,
            text:           form.text.value,
            timeCreated:    moment().unix(),
            author:         user.profile.name,
            owner:          user._id

    }, function(error) {
        if(error) {
            // display the error to the user
            alert(error.reason);
        } else {
            // Redirect to the post
            Router.go('Post', {slug: slug});
        }
    });
    }
});
```

The second argument we pass to the `insert()` function is a callback function provided by Meteor that will receive an error argument if something goes wrong. If an error happens, we alert it, and if everything goes fine, we redirect to the newly inserted post using our generated slug.

Since our route controller will then subscribe to a post with this slug, it will be able to load our newly created post and display it in the post template.

Now, if we go to the browser, fill in the form, and click on the **Save** button, we should have created our first own post!

Editing posts

So saving works. What about editing?

When we click on the **Edit** button in the post, we will be shown the editPost
template again. This time, however, the form fields are filled with the data from
the post. So far so good, but if we press the **Save** button now, we will create another
post instead of updating the current one.

Updating the current post

Since we set the data context of the editPost template, we can simply use the
presence of the post's _id field as an indicator to update, instead of inserting
the post data:

```
Template.editPost.events({
    'submit form': function(e, tmpl){
        e.preventDefault();
        var form = e.target,
            user = Meteor.user(),
            _this = this; // we need this to reference the slug in the
callback

        // Edit the post
        if(this._id) {

            Posts.update(this._id, {$set: {
                title:          form.title.value,
                description:    form.description.value,
                text:           form.text.value

            }}, function(error) {
                if(error) {
                    // display the error to the user
                    alert(error.reason);
                } else {
                    // Redirect to the post
                    Router.go('Post', {slug: _this.slug});
                }
            });

        // SAVE
        } else {

            // The insertion process ...

        }
    }
});
```

Knowing the `_id`, we can simply update the current document using the `$set` property. Using `$set` will only overwrite the `title`, `description`, and `text` fields. The other fields will be left as they are.

Note that we now also need to create the `_this` variable on top of the function in order to access the `slug` property of the current data context in the callback later. This way, we can later redirect to our edited post page.

Now, if we save the file and go back to our browser, we can edit the post and click on **Save**, and all changes will be saved as expected to our database.

Now, we can create and edit posts. In the next section, we will learn how to restrict updates to the database by adding the allow and deny rules.

Restricting database updates

Until now, we simply added the insert and update functionality to our `editPost` template. However, anybody can insert and update data if they just type an `insert` statement into their browser's console.

To prevent this, we need to properly check for insertion and update rights on the server side before updating the database.

Meteor's collections come with the allow and deny functions, which will be run before every insertion or update to determine whether the action is allowed or not.

The allow rules let us allow certain documents or fields to be updated, whereas the deny rules overwrite any allow rules and definitely deny any action on its collection.

To make this more visible, let's visualize an example where we define two allow rules; one will allow certain documents' `title` fields to be changed and another will allow only editing of the `description` fields, but an additional deny rule can prevent one specific document to be edited in any case.

Removing the insecure package

To start using the allow and deny rules, we need to remove the `insecure` package from our app so that no client can simply make changes to our database without passing our allow and deny rules.

Quit the running `meteor` instance using *Ctrl + C* in the terminal and run the following command:

```
$ meteor remove insecure
```

After we have successfully removed the package, we can run Meteor again using the `meteor` command.

When we now go to our browser and try to edit any post, we will see an alert window stating **Access denied**. Remember that we added this `alert()` call before, when an update or insert action failed?

Adding our first allow rules

In order to make our posts editable again, we need to add allow rules to enable database updates again.

To do so, we will add the following allow rules to our `my-meteor-blog/collections.js` file, but in this case we'll execute them only on the server side by checking against Meteor's `isServer` variable, as follows:

```
if(Meteor.isServer) {

    Posts.allow({
        insert: function (userId, doc) {
            // The user must be logged in, and the document must be
owned by the user
            return userId && doc.owner === userId && Meteor.user().
roles.admin;
        },
```

In the insertion *allow* rule , we will insert the document only if the post owner matches the current user and if the user is an admin, which we can determine by the `roles.admin` property we added in the previous chapter.

If the allow rule returns `false`, the insertion of the document will be denied. Otherwise, we will successfully add a new post. Updating works the same way, just that we only check whether the current user is an admin:

```
        update: function (userId, doc, fields, modifier) {
            // User must be an admin
            return Meteor.user().roles.admin;
        },
        // make sure we only get this field from the documents
        fetch: ['owner']
    });
}
```

The arguments passed to the update function are listed in the following table:

Field	Description
userId	The user ID of the current logged-in user, who performs that update action
doc	The document from the database, without the proposed changes
fields	An array with field parameters that will be updated
modifier	The modifier the user passed to the update function, such as {$set: {'name.first': "Alice"}, $inc: {score: 1}}

The fetch property, which we specify last in the allow rule's object, determines which fields of the current document should be passed to the update rule. In our case, we only need the owner property for our update rule. The fetch property exists for performance reasons, to prevent unnecessarily large documents from being passed to the rule's functions.

> Additionally, we can specify the remove() rule and the transform() function. The remove() rule will get the same arguments as the insert() rule and allow or prevent removal of documents.
>
> The transform() function can be used to transform the document before being passed to the allow or deny rules, for example, to normalize it. However, be aware that this won't change the document that gets inserted into the database.

If we now try to edit a post in our website, we should be able to edit all posts as well as create new ones.

Adding a deny rule

To improve security, we can fix the owner of the post and the time when it was created. We can prevent changes to the owner and the timeCreated and slug fields by adding an additional deny rule to our Posts collection, as follows:

```
if(Meteor.isServer) {

  // Allow rules

  Posts.deny({
    update: function (userId, docs, fields, modifier) {
      // Can't change owners, timeCreated and slug
```

```
        return _.contains(fields, 'owner') || _.contains(fields,
  'timeCreated') || _.contains(fields, 'slug');
      }
    });
  }
```

This rule will simply check whether the `fields` argument contains one of the restricted fields. If it does, we deny the update to this post. So, even if our previous allow rules have passed, our deny rule ensures that the document doesn't change.

We can try the deny rule by going to our browser's console, and when we are at a post page, typing the following commands:

```
Posts.update(Posts.findOne()._id, {$set: {'slug':'test'}});
```

This should give you an error stating **update failed: Access denied**, as shown in the following screenshot:

Though we can add and update posts now, there is a better way of adding new posts than simply inserting them into our `Posts` collection from the client side.

Adding posts using a method call

Methods are functions that can be called from the client and will be executed on the server.

Method stubs and latency compensation

The advantage of methods is that they can execute code on the server, having the full database and a stub method on the client available.

For example, we can have a method do something on the server and simulate the expected outcome in a stub method on the client. This way, the user doesn't have to wait for the server's response. A stub can also invoke an interface change, such as adding a loading indicator.

One native example of a method call is Meteor's `Collection.insert()` function, which will execute a client-side function, inserting the document immediately into the local `minimongo` database as well as sending a request executing the real `insert` method on the server. If the insertion is successful, the client has the document already inserted. If an error occurs, the server will respond and remove the inserted document from the client again.

In Meteor, this concept is called **latency compensation**, as the interface reacts immediately to the user's response and therefore compensates the latency, while the server's round trip will happen in the background.

Inserting a post using a method call enables us to simply check whether the slug we want to use for the post already exists in another post. Additionally, we can use the server's time for the `timeCreated` property to be sure we are not using an incorrect user timestamp.

Changing the button

In our example, we will simply use the method stub functionality to change the text of the **Save** button to `Saving...` while we run the method on the server. To do so, perform the following steps:

1. To start, let's first change the **Save** button's static text with a template helper so that we can change it dynamically. Open up `my-meteor-blog/client/templates/editPost.html` and replace the **Save** button code with the following code:

   ```
   <button type="submit" class="save">{{saveButtonText}}</button>
   ```

2. Now open `my-meteor-blog/client/templates/editPost.js` and add the following template helper function at the beginning of the file:

```
Session.setDefault('saveButton', 'Save Post');
Template.editPost.helpers({
  saveButtonText: function(){
    return Session.get('saveButton');
  }
});
```

Here, we return the session variable named `saveButton`, which we set to the default value, `Save Post`, earlier.

Changing the session will allow us to change the text of the **Save** button later while saving the document.

Adding the method

Now that we have a dynamic **Save** button, let's add the actual method to our app. For this, we will create a new file called `methods.js` directly in our `my-meteor-blog` folder. This way, its code will be loaded on the server and the client, which is necessary to execute the method on the client as a stub.

Add the following lines of code to add a method:

```
Meteor.methods({
    insertPost: function(postDocument) {

        if(this.isSimulation) {
            Session.set('saveButton', 'Saving...');
        }
    }
});
```

This will add a method called `insertPost`. Inside this method, the stub functionality is already added by making use of the `isSimulation` property, which is made available in the `this` object of the function by Meteor.

The `this` object also has the following properties:

- `unblock()`: This is a function that when called will prevent the method from blocking other method calls
- `userId`: This contains the current user's ID
- `setUserId()`: This a function to connect the current client with a certain user
- `connection`: This is the connection on the server through which this method is called

If `isSimulation` is set to `true`, the method is not run on the server side but as a stub on the client. Inside this condition, we simply set the `saveButton` session variable to `Saving...` so that the button text will change:

```
Meteor.methods({
    insertPost: function(postDocument) {

        if(this.isSimulation) {

            Session.set('saveButton', 'Saving...');

        } else {
```

To complete the method, we will add the server-side code for post insertion:

```
            var user = Meteor.user();

            // ensure the user is logged in
            if (!user)
            throw new Meteor.Error(401, "You need to login to write a
    post");
```

Here, we get the current user to add the author name and owner ID.

We throw an exception with `new Meteor.Error` if the user is not logged in. This will stop the execution of the method and return an error message we define.

We also search for a post with the given slug. If we find one, we prepend a random string to the slug to prevent duplicates. This makes sure that every slug is unique, and we can successfully route to our newly created post:

```
            if(Posts.findOne({slug: postDocument.slug}))
            postDocument.slug = postDocument.slug +'-'+ Math.random().
    toString(36).substring(3);
```

Before we insert the newly created post, we add `timeCreated` using the `moment` library and the `author` and `owner` properties:

```
            // add properties on the serverside
            postDocument.timeCreated = moment().unix();
            postDocument.author      = user.profile.name;
            postDocument.owner       = user._id;

            Posts.insert(postDocument);
```

After we insert the document, we return the corrected slug, which will then be received in the callback of the method call as the second argument:

```
        // this will be received as the second argument of the method
   callback
        return postDocument.slug;
     }
   }
});
```

Calling the method

Now that we have created our `insertPost` method, we can change the code in the submit event, where we inserted the post earlier in our `editPost.js` file, with a call to our method:

```
var slug = _.slugify(form.title.value);

Meteor.call('insertPost', {
   title:          form.title.value
   slug:           slug,
   description:    form.description.value
   text:           form.text.value,

}, function(error, slug) {
   Session.set('saveButton', 'Save Post');

   if(error) {
     return alert(error.reason);
   }

   // Here we use the (probably changed) slug from the server side
   method
   Router.go('Post', {slug: slug});
});
```

As we can see in the callback of the method call, we route to the newly created post using the `slug` variable we received as the second argument in the callback. This ensures that if the `slug` variable is modified on the server side, we use the modified version to route to the post. Additionally, we reset the `saveButton` session variable to change the text to `Save Post` again.

That's it! Now, we can create a new post and save it using our newly created `insertPost` method. However, editing will still be done from the client side using `Posts.update()`, as we now have allow and deny rules, which make sure that only allowed data is modified.

Summary

In this chapter, we learned how to allow and deny database updates. We set up our own allow and deny rules and saw how methods can improve security by moving sensitive processes to the server side. We also improved our procedure of creating posts by checking whether the slug already exists and adding a simple progress indicator.

If you want to dig deeper into the allow and deny rules or methods, take a look at the following Meteor documentations:

- `http://docs.meteor.com/#/full/allow`
- `http://docs.meteor.com/#/full/deny`
- `https://docs.meteor.com/#/full/methods_header`

You can find this chapter's code examples at `https://www.packtpub.com/books/content/support/17713` or on GitHub at `https://github.com/frozeman/book-building-single-page-web-apps-with-meteor/tree/chapter8`.

In the next chapter, we will make our interface real time by constantly updating the post's timestamps.

Advanced Reactivity

Now our blog is basically complete, as we can create and edit entries. In this chapter, we will make use of Meteor's reactive templates to make our interface timestamps update itself. We will build a reactive object that will rerun the template helper, which displays the time when the blog entries were created. This way, they will always display the correct relative time.

In this chapter, we will cover the following topics:

- Reactive programming
- Rerunning functions manually
- Building a reactive object using the `Tracker` package
- Stopping reactive functions

If you've jumped right into the chapter and want to follow the examples, download the previous chapter's code examples from either the book's web page at https://www.packtpub.com/books/content/support/17713 or from the GitHub repository at https://github.com/frozeman/book-building-single-page-web-apps-with-meteor/tree/chapter8.

These code examples will also contain all the style files, so we don't have to worry about adding CSS code along the way.

Reactive programming

As we already saw throughout the book, Meteor uses something called **reactivity**.

One problem that a developer has to solve when building a software application is the consistency of the data represented in the interface. Most modern applications use something called **Model-View-Controller** (**MVC**), where the controller of a view makes sure that it always represents the current state of the model. The model is mostly a server API or a JSON object in the browser memory.

The most common ways of keeping consistent interfaces are as follows (courtesy: `http://manual.meteor.com`):

- **Poll and diff**: Periodically (for example, every second), fetch the current value of the thing, see whether it's changed, and if so, perform the update.

- **Events**: The thing that can change emits an event when it changes. Another part of the program (often called a controller) arranges to listen for this event, gets the current value, and performs the update when the event fires.

- **Bindings**: Values are represented by objects that implement some interface, such as `BindableValue`. Then, a "bind" method is used to tie two `BindableValues` together so that when one value changes, the other is updated automatically. Sometimes, as a part of setting up the binding, a transformation function can be specified. For example, `Foo` can be bound to `Bar` with the `toUpperCase` transformation function.

These patterns are good, but they still need a lot of code to maintain the consistency of the data represented.

Another pattern, although not yet as commonly used, is **reactive programming**. This pattern is a declarative way of binding data. It means when we use a reactive data source such as a `Session` variable or `Mongo.Collection`, we can be sure that reactive functions or template helpers that use these will rerun as soon as its value changes, always keeping the interface or calculations based on these values updated.

The Meteor manual gives us an example use case where reactive programming comes in handy:

> *Reactive programming is perfect for building user interfaces, because instead of attempting to model all interactions in a single piece of cohesive code, the programmer can express what should happen upon specific changes. The paradigm of responding to a change is simpler to understand than modeling which changes affect the state of the program explicitly.*

> *For example, suppose that we are writing an HTML5 app with a table of items, and the user can click on an item to select it or ctrl-click to select multiple items. We might have an <h1> tag and want the contents of the tag to be equal to the name of the currently selected item, capitalized, or else "Multiple selection" if multiple items are selected. And we might have a set of <tr> tags and want the CSS class on each <tr> tag to be "selected" if the items corresponding to that row is in the set of selected items, or the empty string otherwise.*

To make this example happen in the aforementioned patterns, we can quickly see how complex it gets compared to reactive programming (courtesy: `http://manual.meteor.com`):

- If we use poll and diff, the UI will be unacceptably laggy. After the user clicks, the screen won't actually update until the next polling cycle. Also, we have to store the old selection set and diff it against the new selection set, which is a bit of a hassle.

- If we use events, we have to write some fairly tangled controller code to manually map changes to the selection or to the name of the selected item, onto updates to the UI. For example, when the selection changes, we have to remember to update both the `<h1>` tag and (typically) two affected `<tr>` tags. What's more, when the selection changes, we have to automatically register an event handler on the newly selected item so that we can remember to update `<h1>`. It is difficult to structure clean code and maintain it, especially as the UI is extended and redesigned.

- If we use bindings, we will have to use a complex **domain-specific language (DSL)** to express the complex relationships between the variables. The DSL will have to include indirection (bind the contents of `<h1>` not to the name of any fixed item, but to the item indicated by the current selection), transformation (capitalize the name), and conditionals (if more than one item is selected, show a placeholder string).

With Meteor's reactive template engine, Blaze, we can simply use the {{#each}} block helper to iterate over a list of elements and add some conditions for each element based on user interaction or on an item's property to add a selected class.

If the user now changes the data or the data coming in from the server changes, the interface will update itself to represent the data accordingly, saving us a lot of time and avoiding unnecessary complex code.

The invalidating cycle

One key part of understanding the reactive dependencies is the invalidate cycle.

When we use a reactive data source inside a reactive function, such as Tracker. autorun(function() {...}), the reactive data source itself sees that it is inside a reactive function and adds the current function as a dependency to its dependency store.

Then, when the value of the data source changes, it invalidates (reruns) all its dependent functions and removes them from its dependency store.

In the rerun of the reactive function, it adds the reactive function back to its dependency store so that they will rerun on its next invalidation (value change) again.

This is the key to understand the reactive concept, as we will see in the following example.

Imagine that we have two Session variables set to false:

```
Session.set('first', false);
Session.set('second', false);
```

Moreover, We have the Tracker.autorun() function, which uses both these variables:

```
Tracker.autorun(function(){
    console.log('Reactive function re-run');
    if(Session.get('first')){
        Session.get('second');
    }
});
```

We can now call Session.set('second', true), but the reactive function will not rerun, because it was never called in the first run, as the first session variable was set to false.

If we now call Session.set(first, true), the function will rerun.

Additionally, if we now set `Session.set('second', false)`, it will rerun as well, as in the second rerun, `Session.get('second')` can add this reactive function as a dependency.

Because the reactive data sources source will always remove all dependencies from its store on every invalidation and add them back in the rerun of the reactive function, we can set `Session.set(first, false)` and try to switch it to `Session.set('second', true)`. The function will *not* rerun again, as `Session.get('second')` was never called in this run!

Once we understand this, we can make more fine-grained reactivity, keeping reactive updates to a minimum. The console output of the explanation looks similar to the following screenshot:

Building a simple reactive object

As we saw, a **reactive object** is an object that when used inside a reactive function, will rerun the function when its value changes. The Meteor's `Session` object is one example of a reactive object.

In this chapter, we will build a simple reactive object that will rerun our `{{formatTime}}` template helper at time intervals so that all the relative times are updated correctly.

Meteor's reactivity is made possible through the `Tracker` package. This package is the core of all reactivity and allows us to track dependencies and rerun these whenever we want.

Perform the following steps to build a simple reactive object:

1. To get started, let's add the following code to the `my-meteor-blog/main.js` file:

   ```
   if(Meteor.isClient) {
       ReactiveTimer = new Tracker.Dependency;
   }
   ```

   This will create a variable named `ReactiveTimer` on the client with a new instance of `Tracker.Dependency`.

2. Below the `ReactiveTimer` variable, but still inside the `if(Meteor.isClient)` condition, we will add the following code to rerun all dependencies of our `ReactiveTimer` object every 10 seconds:

   ```
   Meteor.setInterval(function(){
       // re-run dependencies every 10s
       ReactiveTimer.changed();
   }, 10000);
   ```

   The `Meteor.setInterval` will run the function every 10 seconds.

 Meteor comes with its own implementation of `setInterval` and `setTimeout`. Even though they work exactly as their native JavaScript equivalents, Meteor needs these to reference the right timeout/interval for a specific user on the server side.

Meteor comes with its own implementation of `setInterval` and `setTimeout`. Even though they work exactly as their native JavaScript equivalents, Meteor needs these to reference the right timeout/interval for a specific user on the server side.

Inside the interval, we call `ReactiveTimer.changed()`. This will invalidate every dependent function, causing it to rerun.

Rerunning functions

So far, we have no dependency created, so let's do that. Add the following code below `Meteor.setInterval`:

```
Tracker.autorun(function(){
    ReactiveTimer.depend();
    console.log('Function re-run');
});
```

If we now get back to our browser console, we should see **Function re-run** every 10 seconds, as our reactive object reruns the function.

We can even call `ReactiveTimer.changed()` in our browser console and the function will rerun as well.

These are good examples, but don't make our timestamps update automatically.

To do this, we need to open up `my-meteor-blog/client/template-helpers.js` and add the following line at the top of our `formatTime` helper function:

```
ReactiveTimer.depend();
```

This will make every `{{formatTime}}` helper in our app rerun every 10 seconds, updating the relative time while it passes. To see this, go to your browser and create a new blog entry. If you save the blog entry now and watch the time created text, you will see that it changes after a while:

Creating an advanced timer object

The previous example was a simple demonstration of a custom reactive object. To make it more useful, it is better to create a separate object that hides the `Tracker.Dependency` functions and adds additional functionality.

Meteor's reactivity and dependency tracking allows us to create dependencies even when the `depend()` function is called from inside another function. This dependency chain allows more complex reactive objects.

In the next example, we will take our `timer` object and add a `start` and `stop` function to it. Additionally, we will also make it possible to choose a time interval at which the timer will rerun:

1. First, let's remove the previous code examples from the `main.js` and `template-helpers.js` files, which we added before, and create a new file named `ReactiveTimer.js` inside `my-meteor-blog/client` with the following content:

    ```
    ReactiveTimer = (function () {

        // Constructor
        function ReactiveTimer() {
            this._dependency = new Tracker.Dependency;
            this._intervalId = null;
        };

        return ReactiveTimer;
    })();
    ```

    This creates a classic prototype class in JavaScript, which we can instantiate using `new ReactiveTimer()`. In its constructor function, we instantiate a new `Tracker.Dependency` and attach it to the function.

2. Now, we will create a `start()` function, which will start a self-chosen interval:

    ```
    ReactiveTimer = (function () {

        // Constructor
        function ReactiveTimer() {
            this._dependency = new Tracker.Dependency;
            this._intervalId = null;
        };
    ```

```
ReactiveTimer.prototype.start = function(interval){
    var _this = this;
    this._intervalId = Meteor.setInterval(function(){
        // rerun every "interval"
        _this._dependency.changed();
    }, 1000 * interval);
};


    return ReactiveTimer;
})();
```

This is the same code as we used before with the difference that we store the interval ID in `this._intervalId` so that we can stop it later in our `stop()` function. The interval passed to the `start()` function must be in seconds;

3. Next, we add the `stop()` function to the class, which will simply clear the interval:

```
ReactiveTimer.prototype.stop = function(){
    Meteor.clearInterval(this._intervalId);
};
```

4. Now we only need a function that creates the dependencies:

```
ReactiveTimer.prototype.tick = function(){
    this._dependency.depend();
};
```

Our reactive timer is ready!

5. Now, to instantiate the `timer` and start it with whatever interval we like, add the following code after the `ReactiveTimer` class at the end of the file:

```
timer = new ReactiveTimer();
timer.start(10);
```

6. At last, we need to go back to our `{{formatTime}}` helper in the `template-helper.js` file, and `add` the `time.tick()` function, and every relative time in the interface will update as time goes by.

7. To see the reactive timer in action, run the following code snippet in our browser's console:

```
Tracker.autorun(function(){
    timer.tick();
    console.log('Timer ticked!');
});
```

8. We should now see **Timer ticked!** logged every 10 seconds. If we now run `time.stop()`, the timer will stop running its dependent functions. If we call `time.start(2)` again, we will see Timer ticked! now appearing every two seconds, as we set the interval to 2:

As we can see, our `timer` object is now rather flexible, and we can create any number of time intervals to be used throughout the app.

Reactive computations

Meteor's reactivity and the `Tracker` package is a very powerful feature, as it allows event-like behavior to be attached to every function and every template helper. This reactivity is what keeps our interface consistent.

Although we only touched the `Tracker` package until now, it has a few more properties that we should take a look at.

We already learned how to instantiate a reactive object. We can call `new Tracker.Dependency`, which can create and rerun dependencies using `depend()` and `changed()`.

Stopping reactive functions

When we are inside a reactive function, we also have access to the current computational object, which we can use to stop further reactive behavior.

To see this in action, we can use our already running `timer` and create the following reactive function using `Tracker.autorun()` in our browser's console:

```
var count = 0;
var someInnerFunction = function(count){
    console.log('Running for the '+ count +' time');

    if(count === 10)
        Tracker.currentComputation.stop();
};
Tracker.autorun(function(c){
    timer.tick();

    someInnerFunction(count);

    count++;
});

timer.stop();
timer.start(2);
```

Here, we create `someInnerFunction()` to show how we can access the current computation as well from nested functions. In this inner function, we get the computation using `Tracker.currentComputation`, which gives us the current `Tracker.Computation` object.

We use the `count` variable, we created before the `Tracker.autorun()` function, to count up. When we reach 10, we call `Tracker.currentComputation.stop()`, which will stop the dependency of the inner and the `Tracker.autorun()` functions, making them nonreactive.

To see the results quicker, we stop and start the `timer` object with an interval of two seconds at the end of the example.

If we copy and paste the previous code snippet into our browser's console and run it, we should see **Running for the xx time** appearing 10 times:

```
⊘  ▽  <top frame>                          ▼

timer.stop();
timer.start(2);
Running for the 0 time
undefined
Running for the 1 time
Running for the 2 time
Running for the 3 time
Running for the 4 time
Running for the 5 time
Running for the 6 time
Running for the 7 time
Running for the 8 time
Running for the 9 time
Running for the 10 time
>  |
```

The current computational object is useful to give us control over reactive dependencies from inside the dependent functions.

Preventing run at start

The `Tracker .Computation` object also comes with the `firstRun` property, which we have used in an earlier chapter.

Reactive functions, for example, when created using `Tracker.autorun()` also run when they are parsed by JavaScript for the first time. If we want to prevent this, we can simply stop the function before any code is executed when checking whether `firstRun` is `true`:

```
Tracker.autorun(function(c){
    timer.tick();

    if(c.firstRun)
        return;

    // Do some other stuff
});
```

We don't need to get the current computation here using `Tracker.currentComputation`, as `Tracker.autorun()` gets it already as its first argument.

Also, when we stop a `Tracker.autorun()` function, as described in the following code, it will never create the dependency for the session variable, as `Session.get()` was never called in the first run:

```
Tracker.autorun(function(c){
    if(c.firstRun)
        return;

    Session.get('myValue');
}):
```

To make sure that we make the function depending on the `myValue` session variable, we need to put it before the `return` statement.

Advanced reactive objects

The `Tracker` package has a few more advanced properties and functions that allow you to control when dependencies are invalidated (`Tracker.flush()` and `Tracker.Computation.invalidate()`) and allow you to register additional callbacks on it (`Tracker.onInvalidate()`).

These properties allow you to build complex reactive objects, which are out of the scope of this book. If you want to get a deeper understanding of the `Tracker` package, I recommend that you take a look at the Meteor manual at `http://manual.meteor.com/#tracker`.

Summary

In this chapter, we learned how to build our own custom reactive object. We learned about `Tracker.Dependency.depend()` and `Tracker.Dependency.changed()` and saw how reactive dependencies have their own computational objects, which can be used to stop its reactive behavior and prevent running at start.

To dig deeper, take a look at the documentation for the `Tracker` package and see detailed property descriptions for the `Tracker.Computation` object at the following resources:

- `https://www.meteor.com/tracker`
- `https://docs.meteor.com/#/full/tracker`
- `https://docs.meteor.com/#/full/tracker_computation`
- `https://docs.meteor.com/#/full/tracker_dependency`

You can find this chapter's code examples at `https://www.packtpub.com/books/content/support/17713` or on GitHub at `https://github.com/frozeman/book-building-single-page-web-apps-with-meteor/tree/chapter9`.

Now that we have finalized our blog, we will take a look at how to deploy our app on servers in the next chapter.

10
Deploying Our App

Our app is now ready to be deployed. In this chapter, we will see how we can deploy our app on different servers to make it public and show the world what we built.

Meteor makes it easy to deploy applications on its own server infrastructure. It's free and quick to do, but probably not the right place for a production environment. Therefore, we will take a look at manual deployment as well as some great tools built to deploy on any Node.js server.

In this chapter, we will cover the following topics:

- Registering a Meteor developer account
- Deploying on Meteor's own server infrastructure
- Bundling and deploying Meteor manually
- Deploying using Demeteorizer
- Deploying using Meteor Up

If you want to have the full app we've built in this book to deploy, download the code from the book's web page at `https://www.packtpub.com/books/content/support/17713` or from the GitHub repository at `https://github.com/frozeman/book-building-single-page-web-apps-with-meteor/tree/chapter10`.

This code won't have the part where dummy posts are created, so you can have a clean blog to start with on your own server.

Deploying on meteor.com

Meteor provides its own hosting environment, where everybody can deploy apps with a single command, for free. In order to deploy apps, Meteor creates a developer account for us so that we can manage and deploy our apps later. To start, let's perform the following steps to deploy our app on `meteor.com`:

1. Deploying on a subdomain of meteor.com is as simple as running the following command in the terminal from our app's folder:

   ```
   $ meteor deploy myCoolNewBlog
   ```

   We can freely choose the subdomain we want to deploy on. If `myCoolNewBlog.meteor.com` is already taken, Meteor will ask us to log in to the owner's account to overwrite the currently deployed app, or we will have to choose another name.

2. If the domain name is free, Meteor will ask us to provide an e-mail address so that it can create a developer account for us. After entering the e-mail address, we will receive an e-mail with a link to set up our Meteor Developer account, as shown in the following screenshot:

3. To create our account, we need to follow the link given by Meteor so that we can fully set up our account by adding a username and a password, as shown in the next screenshot:

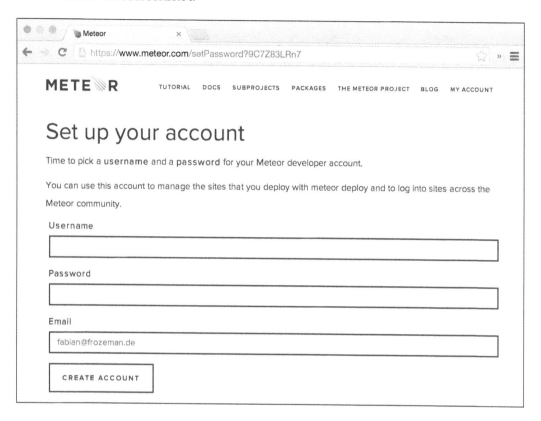

4. After we have done that, we get access to our developer account's page, where we can add e-mail addresses, check our last login, and authorize other Meteor developers to log in to our apps (though we have to add the `accounts-meteor-developer` package first).

5. Now, to finally deploy our app, we need to log in with our Meteor Developer account in the terminal by using $ `meteor login`, entering our credentials, and running the `deploy` command again:

```
$ meteor deploy myCoolNewBlog
```

6. Using the $ meteor authorized -add <username> command, we can allow other Meteor developers to deploy to our app's subdomain, as shown in the following screenshot:

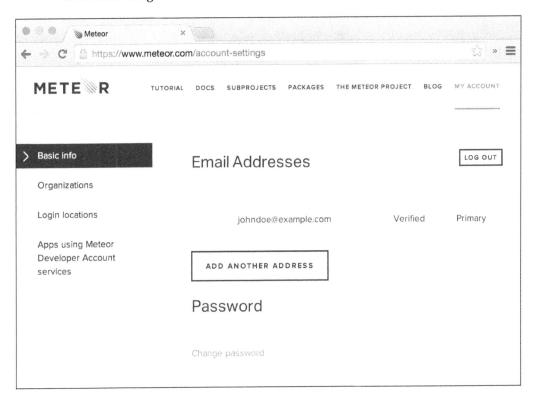

7. If we want to update our deployed app, we can simply run $ meteor deploy from inside our app's folder. Meteor will ask us for our credentials, and we can then deploy our app.

If we're on a friend's computer and want to use our Meteor account, we can do so using $ meteor login. Meteor will keep us logged in and everybody can redeploy any of our apps. We need to make sure we use $ meteor logout when we're finished.

Deploying on meteor.com using a domain name

We can also host our app on `meteor.com`, but can define our own domain name.

To do this, we simply deploy using our domain name, as follows:

```
$ meteor deploy mydomain.com
```

This will host the app on meteor.com, but with no direct URL such as `myapp.meteor.com`.

To point our domain to the app on the Meteor servers, we need to change the **A record** of our domain to the IP address of `origin.meteor.com` (which is `107.22.210.133` at the time of writing this book), or the `CNAME` record to `origin.meteor.com`. You can do this at the provider where you registered your domain under the DNS configuration.

Meteor will then get a request from our domain and redirect internally to the server where our app is located.

Backup and restore databases hosted on meteor.com

If you ever need to back up your database or move it to another server, you can get temporary Mongo database credentials for the deployed database using the following command:

```
$ meteor mongo myapp.meteor.com -url
```

This will get something like the following credentials:

```
mongodb://client-ID:xyz@production-db-b1.meteor.io:27017/yourapp_meteor_com
```

You can then use the credentials from the preceding output to back up your database using `mongodump`:

```
$ mongodump -h production-db-b1.meteor.io --port 27017 --username client-ID --password xyz --db yourapp_meteor_com
```

This will create a folder named `dump/yourapp_meteor_com` where you are and put the dump files of the database inside.

To restore it to another server, use `mongorestore`, with the last argument being the folder where you put the database dump:

```
$ mongorestore -h mymongoserver.com --port 27017 --username myuser
--password xyz --db my_new_database dump/yourapp_meteor_com
```

If you simply want to put the data into your local Meteor app's database, start the Meteor server using `$ meteor` and run the following command:

```
$ mongorestore --port 3001
```

Deploying on other servers

Meteor's free hosting is great, but when it comes to using an app in production, we want to be in control of the server we're using.

Meteor allows us to create a bundle of our application so that we can deploy it on any Node.js server. The only downside to this is that we need to install certain dependencies ourselves. Additionally, there are two packages out there that make deploying apps almost as simple as Meteor itself, though their configuration is still needed.

Bundling our app

In order to deploy our app on our own server, we need to have a Linux server with the latest version of Node.js and NPM installed. The server should have the same platform as our local machine on which we will create the bundle. If you want to deploy your app on another platform, take a look at the next section. Now let's build the app by performing the following steps:

1. If our server fits the aforementioned requirements, we can go to our app's folder on our local machine and run the following command:

   ```
   $ meteor build myAppBuildFolder
   ```

2. This will create `myAppBuildFolder` with a `*.tar.gz` file inside. We can then upload this file to our server and extract it under `~/Sites/myApp` for example. Then we go to the extracted folder and run the following commands:

   ```
   $ cd programs/server
   $ npm install
   ```

3. This will install all the NPM dependencies. After they're installed, we set the necessary environment variables:

```
$ export MONGO_URL='mongodb://user:password@host:port/
databasename'
$ export ROOT_URL='http://example.com'
$ export MAIL_URL='smtp://user:password@mailhost:port/'
$ export PORT=8080
```

The `export` commands will set the `MONGO_URL`, `ROOT_URL`, and `MAIL_URL` environment variables.

4. As this manual deployment doesn't come with preinstalled MongoDB, we need to either install it on our machine or use a hosted service such as Compose (`http://mongohq.com`). If we rather want to install MongoDB on our server ourselves, we can follow the guide at `http://docs.mongodb.org/manual/installation`.

5. The `ROOT_URL` variable should be the URL of the domain pointing to our server. If our app sends e-mails, we can additionally set our own SMTP server or use a service such as Mailgun (`http://mailgun.com`) and change the SMTP host in the `MAIL_URL` variable.

   We can also specify the port on which we want our app to run using the `PORT` environment variable. If we don't set the `PORT` variable, it will use port `80` by default.

6. After we set these variables, we go to the root folder of our app and start the server using the following command:

```
$ node main.js
```

 If you want to make sure your application is restarted in case it crashes or when the server is rebooted, take a look at the `forever` NPM package, which is explained at `https://github.com/nodejitsu/forever`.

If everything goes fine, our app should be reachable at `<your server's ip>:8080`.

In case we run into trouble by manually deploying our app, we can use the next approach.

Deploying using Demeteorizer

The disadvantage of using `$ meteor build` is that most node modules are already compiled, and therefore can cause problems in the server's environment. Hence comes Demeteorizer, which is very similar to `$ meteor build` but will additionally unpack the bundle and create a `package.json` file with all the node dependencies and the correct node version for the project. Here is how we deploy using Demeteorizer:

1. Demeteorizer comes as an NPM package, which we can install using the following command:

   ```
   $ npm install -g demeteorizer
   ```

    If the npm folder doesn't have the right permissions, use `sudo` before the command.

2. Now we can go to our app's folder and type the following command:

   ```
   $ demeteorizer -o ~/my-meteor-blog-converted
   ```

3. This will output the ready-to-distribute app to the `my-meteor-blog-converted` folder. We just copy this folder to our server, set the same environment variables as described earlier, and run the following command:

   ```
   $ cd /my/server/my-meteor-blog-converted
   $ npm install
   $ node main.js
   ```

This should start our app on the port we specified.

Deploying using Meteor Up

The previous steps help us to deploy our app on our own server, but this method still requires us to build, upload, and set the environment variables.

Meteor Up (mup) aims to make deploying as easy as running `$ meteor deploy`. However, if we want to use Meteor Up, we need to have full admin rights on the server.

Additionally, this allows us to auto-restart the app in case it crashes, using the `forever` NPM package, as well as start the app when the server reboots, using the `upstart` NPM package. We can also revert to the previously deployed version, which gives us a good basis for deployment on the production environment.

The next steps are for more advanced developers, as they require setting up `sudo` rights on the server machine. Therefore, if you're inexperienced in deployment, consider using a service such as Modulus (`http://modulus.io`), which offers online Meteor deployment using its own command-line tool, available at `https://modulus.io/codex/meteor_apps`.

Meteor Up will set up the server and deploy our app as follows:

1. To install `mup` on our local machine, we type the following command:

   ```
   $ npm install -g mup
   ```

2. Now we need to create a folder for our deployment configuration, which could be in the same folder where our app is located:

   ```
   $ mkdir ~/my-meteor-blog-deployment
   $ cd ~/my-meteor-blog-deployment
   $ mup init
   ```

3. Meteor Up creates a configuration file for us, which will look like the following:

   ```
   {
     "servers": [
       {
         "host": "hostname",
         "username": "root",
         "password": "password"
         // or pem file (ssh based authentication)
         //"pem": "~/.ssh/id_rsa"
       }
     ],
     "setupMongo": true,
     "setupNode": true,
     "nodeVersion": "0.10.26",
     "setupPhantom": true,
     "appName": "meteor",
     "app": "/Users/arunoda/Meteor/my-app",
     "env": {
       "PORT": 80,
       "ROOT_URL": "http://myapp.com",
       "MONGO_URL": "mongodb://arunoda:fd8dsjsfh7@hanso.mongohq.
   com:10023/MyApp",
       "MAIL_URL": "smtp://postmaster%40myapp.mailgun.
   org:adj87sjhd7s@smtp.mailgun.org:587/"
     },
     "deployCheckWaitTime": 15
   }
   ```

4. Now we can edit this file to work for our server environment.

5. First, we will add the SSH server authentication. We can provide either our RSA key file or a username and a password. If we want to use the latter, we need to install `sshpass`, a tool used to provide SSH passwords without using the command line:

```
"servers": [
    {
        "host": "myServer.com",
        "username": "johndoe",
        "password": "xyz"
        // or pem file (ssh based authentication)
        //"pem": "~/.ssh/id_rsa"
    }
],
```

 To install `sshpass` for our environment, we can follow the steps at `https://gist.github.com/arunoda/7790979`, or if you're on Mac OS X, take a look at `http://www.hashbangcode.com/blog/installing-sshpass-osx-mavericks`.

6. Next, we can set some options, such as choosing to install MongoDB on the server. If we use a service such as Compose, we will set it to `false`:

```
"setupMongo": false,
```

If we already have Node.js installed on our server, we will also set the next option to `false`:

```
"setupNode": false,
```

If we want to mention a specific Node.js version, we can set it as follows:

```
"nodeVersion": "0.10.25",
```

Meteor Up can also install PhantomJS for us, which is necessary if we use Meteor's spiderable package, which makes our app crawlable by search engines:

```
"setupPhantom": true,
```

In the next option, we will set the name of our app, which can be the same as our app's folder name:

```
"appName": "my-meteor-blog",
```

Finally, we point to our local app folder so that Meteor Up knows what to deploy:

```
"app": "~/my-meteor-blog",
```

7. Meteor Up also lets us preset all the necessary environment variables, such as the correct `MONGO_URL` variable:

```
"env": {
    "ROOT_URL": "http://myServer.com",
    "MONGO_URL": "mongodb://user:password@host:port/databasename",
    "PORT": 8080
},
```

8. The last option sets the time Meteor Up will wait for before checking whether the app started successfully:

```
"deployCheckWaitTime": 15
```

Setting up the server

In order to set up the server using Meteor Up, we need a no-password access to sudo. Perform the following steps to set up the server:

1. To enable no-password access, we need to add our current user to the server's sudo group:

```
$ sudo adduser <username> sudo
```

2. Then add NOPASSWD to the sudoers file:

```
$ sudo visudo
```

3. Now replace the %sudo ALL=(ALL) ALL line with the following line:

```
%sudo ALL=(ALL) NOPASSWD:ALL
```

Deploying with mup

If everything has worked fine, we can set up our server. The following steps explain how we can deploy with mup:

1. Run the following command from inside the local `my-meteor-blog-deployment` folder:

```
$ mup setup
```

This will configure our server and install all requirements chosen in our configuration file.

Once this process is done, we can deploy our app any time by running the following command from the same folder:

```
$ mup deploy
```

This way, we can also create production and staging environments by creating two separate Meteor Up configurations with two distinct app names, and deploy it to the same server.

Outlook

Currently, Meteor limits native deployment to its own servers, with limited control over the environment. Planned is an enterprise-grade server infrastructure called **Galaxy**, which will make deploying and scaling Meteor apps as simple as Meteor itself.

Nonetheless, with Meteor's simplicity and great community, we already have a rich set of tools available to deploy to any Node.js-based hosting and PaaS environment.

 For example, if we wanted to deploy on Heroku, we can take a look at the build pack by Jordan Sissel at `https://github.com/jordansissel/heroku-buildpack-meteor`.

Summary

In this chapter, we learned how to deploy Meteor and how simple deploying on Meteor's own server infrastructure can be. We also used tools such as Demeteorizer and Meteor Up to deploy on our own server infrastructure.

To read more about the specific deployment methods, take a look at the following resources:

- `https://www.meteor.com/services/developer-accounts`
- `https://docs.meteor.com/#/full/deploying`
- `https://www.meteor.com/services/build`
- `https://github.com/onmodulus/demeteorizer`
- `https://github.com/arunoda/meteor-up`

You can find the full example code of this app, ready for deployment, at `https://www.packtpub.com/books/content/support/17713` or on GitHub at `https://github.com/frozeman/book-building-single-page-web-apps-with-meteor/tree/chapter10`.

In the next chapter, we will create a package of our previously created `ReactiveTimer` object and publish it to Meteor's official package repository.

11

Building Our Own Package

In this chapter, we will learn how to build our own package. Writing packages allows us to create closed-functionality components that can be shared between many apps. In the second half of the chapter, we will publish our app on Atmosphere, Meteor's third-party package repository, at `https://atmospherejs.com`.

In this chapter, we will cover the following topics:

- Structuring a package
- Creating a package
- Publishing your own package

> In this chapter, we will package the `ReactiveTimer` object that we built in *Chapter 9, Advanced Reactivity*. To follow the examples in this chapter, download the previous chapter's code examples from either the book's web page at `https://www.packtpub.com/books/content/support/17713` or from the GitHub repository at `https://github.com/frozeman/book-building-single-page-web-apps-with-meteor/tree/chapter10`.

The structure of a package

A package is a bundle of JavaScript files that exposes only specific variables to a Meteor app. Other than in a Meteor app, package files will get loaded in the loading order we specify.

Every package needs a `package.js` file that contains the configuration of that package. In such a file, we can add a name, description, and version, set the loading order, and determine which variables should be exposed to the app. Additionally, we can specify unit tests for our packages to test them.

An example of a `package.js` file can look like this:

```
Package.describe({
  name: "mrt:moment",
  summary: "Moment.js, a JavaScript date library.",
  version: "0.0.1",
  git: "https://..."
});

Package.onUse(function (api, where) {
  api.export('moment');

  api.addFiles('lib/moment-with-langs.min.js', 'client');
});

Package.onTest(function(api){
  api.use(["mrt:moment", "tinytest"], ["client", "server"]);
  api.addFiles("test/tests.js", ["client", "server"]);
});
```

We can structure the files and folders in our package as we wish, but a good basis is the following arrangement:

- `tests`: This contains the package's unit tests and the `tests.js` file
- `lib`: This contains third-party libraries used by the package
- `README.md`: This contains simple instructions on how to use the package
- `package.js`: This contains the package's metadata
- `myPackage.js`: These are one or more files that contain the package code

To test a package, we can use Meteor's `tinytest` package, which is a simple unit testing package. If we have tests, we can run them using the following command:

```
$ meteor test-packages <my package name>
```

This will start a Meteor app at `http://localhost:3000`, which runs our package tests. To see how to write a package, take a look at the next chapter.

Creating our own package

To create our own package, we will use our `ReactiveTimer` object, which we built in *Chapter 9, Advanced Reactivity*:

1. We go to our terminal, in our app's folder and run the following command:

    ```
    $ meteor create --package reactive-timer
    ```

2. This will create a folder named `packages` with a `reactive-timer` folder inside it. Inside the `reactive-timer` folder, Meteor has already created a `package.js` file and some example package files.

3. Now we can delete all the files inside the `reactive-timer` folder, except the `package.js` file.

4. Then we move the `my-meteor-blog/client/ReactiveTimer.js` file, which we created in *Chapter 9, Advanced Reactivity*, to our newly created `reactive-timer` package folder.

5. Lastly, we open the copied `ReactiveTimer.js` file and remove the following lines:

    ```
    timer = new ReactiveTimer();
    timer.start(10);
    ```

    Later, we'll instantiate the `timer` object inside the app itself and not in the package file.

We should now have a simple folder with the default `package.js` file and our `ReactiveTimer.js` file. This is almost it! We just need to configure our package and we are ready to use it in our app.

Adding the package metadata

To add the package's metadata, we open the file called `package.js` and add the following lines of code:

```
Package.describe({
  name: "meteor-book:reactive-timer",
  summary: "A simple timer object, which can re-run reactive functions
based on an interval",
  version: "0.0.1",
  // optional
  git: "https://github.com/frozeman/meteor-reactive-timer"
});
```

This adds a name to the package as well as a description and a version.

Note that the package name is namespaced with the author's name. This exists so that packages with the same name can be made distinct through the names of their authors. In our case, we choose meteor-book, which is not a real username. To publish the package, we need to use our real Meteor developer username.

After the Package.describe() function come the actual package dependencies:

```
Package.onUse(function (api) {
  // requires Meteor core packages 1.0
  api.versionsFrom('METEOR@1.0');

  // we require the Meteor core tracker package
  api.use('tracker', 'client');

  // and export the ReactiveTimer variable
  api.export('ReactiveTimer');

  // which we find in this file
  api.addFiles('ReactiveTimer.js', 'client');
});
```

Here, we define the version of the Meteor core packages this package should use:

- With api.use(), we define an additional package (or packages) this package depends on. Note that these dependencies won't be accessible to the app itself, which uses this package.

> Additionally, there exists api.imply(), which not only makes another package available in the package's files, but also adds it to the Meteor app itself so that it can be accessed by the app's code.

- If we use a third-party package, we must specify the minimum package version as follows:

```
api.use('author:somePackage@1.0.0', 'server');
```

> We can also pass in a third parameter, {weak: true}, to specify that the dependent package will only be used if it is already added to the app by the developer. This can be used to enhance a package when other packages are present.

- In the second parameter of the `api.use()` function, we can specify whether to load it on the client, server, or both, using an array:

```
api.use('tracker', ['client', 'server']);
```

 We don't really need to import the `Tracker` package, as it's already a part of Meteor's core `meteor-platform` package (added by default to any Meteor app); we do this here for the sake of an example.

- We then use `api.export('ReactiveTimer')` to define which variable of the package should be exposed to the Meteor app using this package. Remember that we created the `ReactiveTimer` object inside the `ReactiveTimer.js` file using the following lines of code:

```
ReactiveTimer = (function () {
  ...
})();
```

 Note that we didn't use `var` to create the variable. This way, it is accessible in all the other files of the package and can also be exposed to the app itself.

- Lastly, we tell the package system which files belong to the package, using `api.addFiles()`. We can have multiple calls of `api.addFiles()` one after the other. This order will then specify the loading order of the files.

  Here, we can again tell Meteor where to load the file — on the client, the server, or both — using `['client', 'server']`.

  In this case, we only provide the `ReactiveTimer` object on the client, as Meteor's reactive functions exist only on the client side.

   If you want to see a full list of methods on the `api` object, take a look at Meteor's documentation at `http://docs.meteor.com/#packagejs`.

Adding the package

Copying a package folder to the `my-meteor-blog/packages` folder is not enough to tell Meteor to use the package. There are additional steps that we need to follow:

1. To add the package, we need to go to our app's folder from the terminal, quit any currently running `meteor` instance, and run the following command:

   ```
   $ meteor add meteor-book:reactive-timer
   ```

2. We then need to instantiate the `ReactiveTimer` object in our app. To do this, we add the following lines of code to our `my-meteor-blog/main.js` file:

   ```
   if(Meteor.isClient) {
       timer = new ReactiveTimer();
       timer.start(10);
   }
   ```

3. Now we can start the Meteor app again using `$ meteor` and open our browser at `http://localhost:3000`.

We shouldn't see any difference, as we just replaced the `ReactiveTimer` object that was already there in our app with the `ReactiveTimer` object from our `meteor-book:reactive-timer` package.

To see the timer run, we can open our browser's console and run the following code snippet:

```
Tracker.autorun(function(){
    timer.tick();
    console.log('timer run');
});
```

This should log `timer run` every 10 seconds, showing us that the package is actually working.

Releasing our package to the public

It's very easy to release a package to the world, but for people to use our package, we should add a readme file so they can know how to use our package.

Create a file called `README.md` in the package folder we created earlier and add the following code snippet:

```
# ReactiveTimer

This package can run reactive functions in a given interval.
```

```
## Installation

    $ meteor add meteor-book:reactive-timer

## Usage

To use the timer, instantiate a new interval:

    var myTimer = new ReactiveTimer();

Then you can start an interval of 10 seconds using:

    myTimer.start(10);

To use the timer just call the following in any reactive function:

    myTimer.tick();

To stop the timer use:

    myTimer.stop();
```

As we can see, this file uses the markdown syntax. This way, it will look good on GitHub and `http://atmospherejs.com`, which is the website where you can browse all the available Meteor packages.

With this readme file, we will make it easy for other people to use the package and appreciate our work.

Publishing our package online

After we have saved the readme file, we can push the package to GitHub or any other online Git repository, and add the repository's URL to the `Package.describe({git: …})` variable of `package.js`. Keeping the code on GitHub keeps it safe and allows others to fork and improve it. Let's perform the following steps to push our package online:

1. To publish our package, we can simply run the following command from inside the `pages` folder in the terminal:

   $ meteor publish --create

   This will build and bundle the package and upload it to Meteor's package servers.

2. If everything goes fine, we should be able to find our package by typing the following command:

```
$ meteor search reactive-timer
```

This is illustrated in the following screenshot:

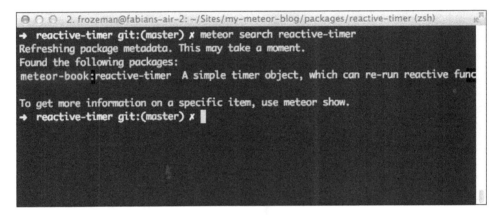

3. We can then show all of the information about the found package using the following command:

```
$ meteor show meteor-book:reactive-timer
```

This is illustrated in the following screenshot:

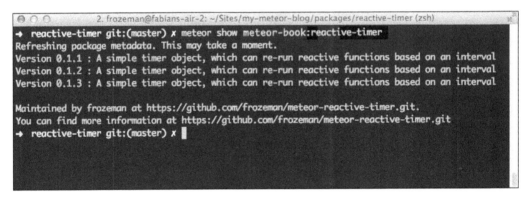

4. To use the package version from the Meteor server, we can simply move the `packages/reactive-timer` folder somewhere else, remove the `package` folder, and run `$ meteor` to start the app.

Now Meteor won't find any package with that name in the `packages` folder and will look online for that package. Since we published it, it will be downloaded and used in our app.

5. Should we want to use a specific version of our package in the app, we can run the following command from inside our app's folder in the terminal:

```
$ meteor add meteor-book:reactive-timer@=0.0.1
```

Now our package is released and we can see it on Atmosphere at
`http://atmospherejs.com/meteor-book/reactive-timer`, as shown
in the following screenshot:

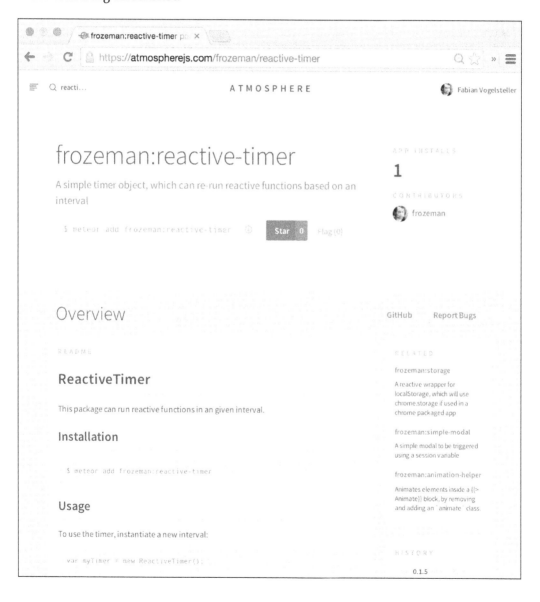

Note that this is just an example of a package and was never actually released. However, a published version of this package under my name can be found at `http://atmospherejs.com/frozeman/reactive-timer`.

Updating our package

If we want to release a new version of our package, we can simply increase the version number in the `package.js` file and publish a new version using the following command from inside the `packages` folder:

```
$ meteor publish
```

To make our app use the latest version of our package (as long as we didn't specify a fixed version), we can simply run the following command from inside our app's folder:

```
$ meteor update meteor-book:reactive-timer
```

If we want to update all packages, we can run the following command:

```
$ meteor update --packages-only
```

Summary

In this chapter, we created our own package from our `ReactiveTimer` object. We also learned how simple it is to publish a package on Meteor's official packaging system.

To dig deeper, read the documentations at the following resources:

- `https://docs.meteor.com/#/full/writingpackages`
- `https://docs.meteor.com/#packagejs`
- `https://www.meteor.com/services/package-server`
- `https://www.meteor.com/isobuild`

You can find this chapter's code examples at `https://www.packtpub.com/books/content/support/17713` or on GitHub at `https://github.com/frozeman/book-building-single-page-web-apps-with-meteor/tree/chapter11`.

This code example contains only the package, so in order to add it to the app, use the code example of the previous chapter.

In the next chapter, we will take a look at testing our app and package.

12
Testing in Meteor

In this final chapter, we will discuss how we can test a Meteor app.

Testing is a comprehensive topic and it goes beyond the scope of this chapter. To keep it simple, we will briefly cover two tools available, as they are certainly different, and show a simple example for each.

In this chapter, we will cover the following topics:

- Testing the `reactive-timer` package
- Using Jasmine to conduct unit tests on our app
- Using Nightwatch to conduct acceptance tests on our app

 If you want to jump right into the chapter and follow the examples, download the code of *Chapter 10, Deploying Our App*, which contains the finished example app, either from the book's web page at https://www.packtpub.com/books/content/support/17713 or from the GitHub repository at https://github.com/frozeman/book-building-single-page-web-apps-with-meteor/tree/chapter10.

Types of tests

Tests are pieces of code that test other pieces of code or functionality of an app.

We can divide tests into four general groups:

- **Unit test**: In this test, we test only a small unit of our code. This can, for example, be a function or a piece of code. Unit tests should not call other functions, write to the hard disk or database, or access the network. If such functionality is needed, one should write stubs, which are functions that return the expected value without calling the real function.

- **Integrations test**: In this test, we combine multiple tests and run them in different environments to make sure that they still work. The difference in this test compared to the unit test is that we are actually running connected functionalities, such as calling the database.

- **Functional test**: This can be a unit test or tests in the interface, but will only test the functionality of a feature/function without checking for side effects, such as whether or not variables were cleaned up properly.

- **Acceptance test**: This runs tests on the full system, which can, for example, be a web browser. The idea is to mimic the actual user as much as possible. These tests are very similar to user stories that define a feature. The downside is that they make it hard to track down bugs, as the test occurs on a higher level.

In the following examples, we will mostly write functional tests for simplicity.

Testing packages

In the previous chapter, we built a package out of the `ReactiveTimer` object. A good package should always contain unit tests so that people can run them and be sure that changes to that package don't break its functionality.

Meteor provides a simple unit test tool for packages, called `TinyTest`, which we will use to test our package:

1. To add tests, we need to copy the `meteor-book:reactive-timer` package, which we built in the previous chapter, to the `my-meteor-blog/packages` folder of our app. This way, we can make changes to the package, as Meteor will prefer the package in the `packages` folder over one in its package servers. If you removed the package, simply add it back using the following command:

   ```
   $ meteor add meteor-book:reactive-timer
   ```

    Additionally, we need to make sure we delete the `my-meteor-blog/client/ReactiveTimer.js` file, which we should have if we used the code example from *Chapter 10, Deploying Our App*, as a basis.

2. Then we open the `package.js` file from our `packages` folder and add the following lines of code to the end of the file:

   ```
   Package.onTest(function (api) {
     api.use('meteor-book:reactive-timer', 'client');
   ```

```
api.use('tinytest', 'client');

api.addFiles('tests/tests.js', 'client');
});
```

This will include our `meteor-book:reactive-timer` package and `tinytest` when running tests. It will then run the `tests.js` file, which will contain our unit tests.

3. Now, we can create the tests by adding a folder called `tests` to our package's folder and create a file called `tests.js` inside.

Currently, the `tinytest` package is not documented by Meteor, but it is tiny, which means it is very simple.

Basically, there are two functions, `Tinytest.add(test)` and `Tinytest.addAsync(test, expect)`. They both run a simple test function, which we can pass or fail using `test.equal(x, y)`, `test.isTrue(x)`, or `test.isUndefined(x)`.

For our package tests, we will simply test whether `ReactiveTimer._intervalId` is not null after we started the timer, and we will know whether the timer runs or not.

Adding package tests

The test is built by first describing what will be tested.

To test for `_intervalId`, we add the following lines of code to our `tests.js` file:

```
Tinytest.add('The timer set the _intervalId property', function (test)
{
    var timer = new ReactiveTimer();
    timer.start(1);

    test.isTrue(timer._intervalId !== null);

    timer.stop();
});
```

Then we start a timer and test whether its `_intervalId` property is not null anymore. At the end, we stop the timer again to clean up the test.

The next test we will add to our `tests.js` file will be asynchronous, as we need to wait for the timer to run at least once:

```
Tinytest.addAsync('The timer run', function (test, expect) {
    var run = false,
        timer = new ReactiveTimer();
    timer.start(1);

    Tracker.autorun(function(c){
        timer.tick();

        if(!c.firstRun)
            run = true;
    });

    Meteor.setTimeout(function(){
        test.equal(run, true);
        timer.stop();

        expect();
    }, 1010);
});
```

Let's take a look at what is happening in this asynchronous test:

- First, we started the timer again with an interval of 1 second and created a variable called `run`. We then switched this variable to `true` only when our reactive `Tracker.autorun()` function ran. Note that we used `if(!c.firstRun)` to prevent the `run` variable from being set when the function runs the first it's executed, as we only want the "tick" after 1 second to count.

- We then used the `Meteor.setTimeout()` function to check whether `run` was changed to `true`. The `expect()` tells `Tinytest.addAsync()` that the test is over and outputs the result. Note that we also stopped the timer, as we always need to clean up after each test.

Running the package tests

To finally run the test, we can run the following command from our app's root folder:

```
$ meteor test-packages meteor-book:reactive-timer
```

This will start a Meteor app and run our package tests. To see them, we navigate to `http://localhost:3000`:

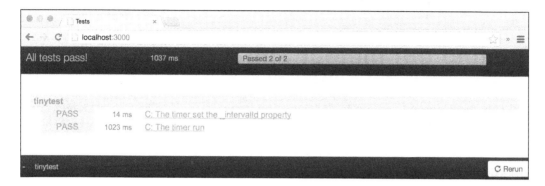

 We can also run a test for more than one package at the same time by naming multiple packages separated by spaces:

```
$ meteor test-packages meteor-book:reactive-timer
iron:router
```

To see if the test works, we will deliberately make it fail by commenting out `Meteor.setInterval()` in the `my-meteor-book/packages/reactive-timer/ReactiveTimer.js` file, as shown in the following screenshot:

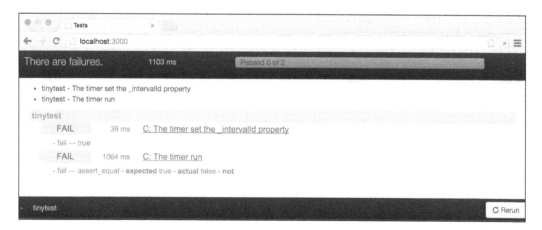

We should always try to make our test fail, as a test could also be written in a way that it never succeeds or fails (for example, when `expect()` was never called). This would stop the execution of other tests, as the current one could never finish.

A good rule of thumb is to test functionality as if we are looking at a black box. If we customize our tests too much depending on how a function is written, we will have a hard time fixing tests as we improve our functions.

Testing our meteor app

To test the app itself, we can use Velocity Meteor's official testing framework.

Velocity itself doesn't contain tools for testing, but rather gives testing packages such as Jasmine or Mocha a unified way to test Meteor apps and report their output in the console or the apps interface itself using the `velocity:html-reporter` package.

Let's quote their own words:

> *Velocity watches your tests/ directory and sends test files to the correct testing plugin. The testing plugin performs the tests and sends results for each test back to Velocity as they complete. Velocity then combines the results from all of the testing plugins and outputs them via one or more reporting plugins. When the app or tests change, Velocity will rerun your tests and reactively update the results.*

This is taken from `http://velocity.meteor.com`. Additionally, Velocity adds features such as Meteor stubs and automatic stubbing. It can create mirror apps for isolated testing and run setup code (fixtures).

We will now take a look at unit and integration tests using Jasmine and acceptance tests using Nightwatch.

Testing using Jasmine

To use Jasmine with Velocity, we need to install the `sanjo:jasmine` package along with the `velocity:html-reporter` package.

To do this, we'll run the following command from inside our apps folder:

```
$ meteor add velocity:html-reporter
```

Then we install Jasmine for Meteor using the following command:

```
$ meteor add sanjo:jasmine
```

In order that Velocity can find the tests, we need to create the following folder structure:

```
- my-meteor-blog
  - tests
```

```
- jasmine
- client
    - unit
    - integration
- server
    - unit
```

Now, when we start the Meteor server using $ meteor, we will see that the Jasmine package has already created two files in the /my-meteor-blog/tests/jasmine/ server/unit folder, which contains stubs for our packages.

Adding unit tests to the server

Now we can add unit tests to the client and the server. In this book, we will only add a unit test to the server and later add integration tests to the client to stay within the scope of this chapter. The steps to do so are as follows:

1. First, we create a file called postSpecs.js within the /my-meteor-blog/ tests/jasmine/server/unit folder and add the following command:

    ```
    describe('Post', function () {
    ```

    This will create a test frame describing what the test inside will be about.

2. Inside the test frame, we call the beforeEach() and afterEach() functions, which will run before and after each test, respectively. Inside, we will create stubs for all Meteor functions using MeteorStubs.install() and clean them afterwards using MeteorStubs.uninstall():

    ```
    beforeEach(function () {
        MeteorStubs.install();
    });

    afterEach(function () {
        MeteorStubs.uninstall();
    });
    ```

A stub is a function or object that mimics its original function or object, but doesn't run actual code. Instead, a stub can be used to return a specific value that the function we test depends on.

Stubbing makes sure that a unit test tests only a specific unit of code and not its dependencies. Otherwise, a break in a dependent function or object would cause a chain of other tests to fail, making it hard to find the actual problem.

3. Now we can write the actual test. In this example, we will test whether the `insertPost` method we created previously in the book inserts the post, and makes sure that no duplicate slug will be inserted:

```
it('should be correctly inserted', function() {

    spyOn(Posts, 'findOne').and.callFake(function() {
        // simulate return a found document;
        return {title: 'Some Tite'};
    });


    spyOn(Posts, 'insert');

    spyOn(Meteor, 'user').and.returnValue({_id: 4321, profile:
{name: 'John'}});

    spyOn(global, 'moment').and.callFake(function() {
        // simulate return the moment object;
        return {unix: function(){
            return 1234;
        }};
    });
});
```

First, we create stubs for all the functions we are using inside the `insertPost` method to make sure that they return what we want.

Especially, take a look at the `spyOn(Posts, "findOne")` call. As we can see, we call a fake function and return a fake document with just a title. Actually, we can return anything as the `insertPost` method only checks whether a document with the same slug was found or not.

4. Next, we actually call the method and give it some post data:

```
Meteor.call('insertPost', {
    title: 'My Title',
    description: 'Lorem ipsum',
    text: 'Lorem ipsum',
    slug: 'my-title'
}, function(error, result){
```

5. Inside the callback of the method, we add the actual tests:

```
expect(error).toBe(null);

// we check that the slug is returned
```

```
        expect(result).toContain('my-title');
        expect(result.length).toBeGreaterThan(8);

        // we check that the post is correctly inserted
        expect(Posts.insert).toHaveBeenCalledWith({
            title: 'My Title',
            description: 'Lorem ipsum',
            text: 'Lorem ipsum',
            slug: result,
            timeCreated: 1234,
            owner: 4321,
            author: 'John'
        });
    });
});
```

First, we check whether the error object is null. Then we check whether the resultant slug of the method contains the `'my-title'` string. Because we returned a fake document in the `Posts.findOne()` function earlier, we expect our method to add some random number to the slug such as `'my-title-fotvadydf4rt3xr'`. Therefore, we check whether the length is bigger than the eight characters of the original `'my-title'` string.

At last, we check whether the `Post.insert()` function was called with the expected values.

To fully understand how you can test Jasmine, take a look at the documentation at `https://jasmine.github.io/2.0/introduction.html`.

You can also find a good cheat sheet of Jasmine functions at `http://www.cheatography.com/citguy/cheat-sheets/jasmine-js-testing`.

6. Finally, we close the `describe(...` function at the beginning:

```
});
```

If we now start our Meteor app again using `$ meteor`, after a while we'll see a green dot appearing in the top-right corner.

Clicking on this dot gives us access to Velocity's `html-reporter` and it should show us that our test has passed:

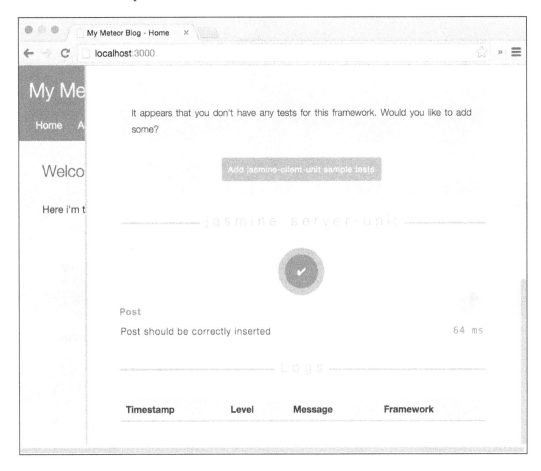

To make our test fail, let's go to our `my-meteor-blog/methods.js` file and comment out the following lines:

```
if(Posts.findOne({slug: postDocument.slug}))
    postDocument.slug = postDocument.slug +'-'+ Math.random().
toString(36).substring(3);
```

This will prevent the slug from getting changed, even if a document with the same slug already exists, and fail our test. If we go back and check in our browser, we should see the test as failed:

We can add more tests by just adding a new `it('should be xyz', function() {...});` function.

Adding integration tests to the client

Adding integration tests is as simple as adding unit tests. The difference is that all the test specification files go to the `my-meteor-blog/tests/jasmine/client/integration` folder.

Integration tests, unlike unit tests, run in the actual app environment.

Adding a test for the visitors

In our first example test, we will test to ensure that visitors can't see the **Create Post** button. In the second test, we will log in as an administrator and check whether we are able to see it.

1. Let's create a file named `postButtonSpecs.js` in our `my-meteor-blog/tests/jasmine/client/integration` folder.

2. Now we add the following code snippet to the file and save it:

```
describe('Vistors', function() {
    it('should not see the create posts link', function () {
        var div = document.createElement('DIV');
        Blaze.render(Template.home, div);

        expect($(div).find('a.createNewPost')[0]).not.
toBeDefined();
    });
});
```

Here we manually create a `div` HTML element and render the `home` template inside. After that, we check whether the `a.createNewPost` link is present.

If we go back to our app, we should see the integration test added and passed:

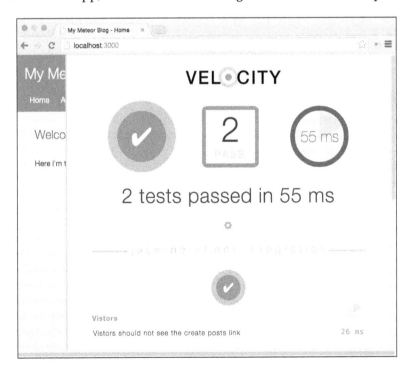

In case the test doesn't show up, just quit and restart the Meteor app in the terminal again.

Adding a test for the admin

In the second test, we will first log in as administrator and then check again whether the button is visible.

We add the following code snippet to the same postButtonSpecs.js file as the one we used before:

```
describe('The Admin', function() {
    afterEach(function (done) {
        Meteor.logout(done);
    })

    it('should be able to login and see the create post link',
function (done) {
        var div = document.createElement('DIV');
        Blaze.render(Template.home, div);

        Meteor.loginWithPassword('johndoe@example.com', '1234',
function (err) {

            Tracker.afterFlush(function(){

                expect($(div).find('a.createNewPost')[0]).toBeDefined();
                expect(err).toBeUndefined();

                done();
            });

        });
    });
});
```

Here we add the home template to a div again, but this time we log in as an admin user, using our admin credentials. After we have logged in, we call Tracker. afterFlush() to give Meteor time to re-render the template and then check whether the button is now present.

Because this test runs asynchronously, we need to call the done() function, which we passed as an argument to the it() function, telling Jasmine that the test is over.

Our credentials inside the test file are secure, as Meteor doesn't bundle files in the `tests` directory.

If we now go back to our browser, we should see the two integration tests as passed:

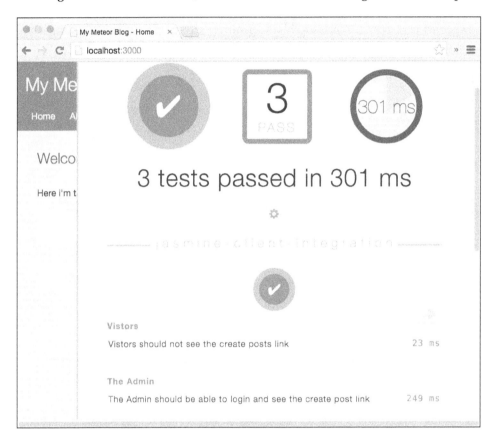

After creating a test, we should always make sure we try to fail the test to see whether it actually works. To do so, we can simply comment out the `a.createNewPost` link in `my-meteor-blog/client/templates/home.html`.

 You can run Velocity tests using PhantomJS as follows:

$ meteor run --test

You first need to install PhantomJS globally with `$ npm install -g phantomjs`. Be aware that this feature is experimental at the time of writing this book and might not run all your tests.

Acceptance tests

Though we can test client and server code separately with these tests, we can't test the interaction between the two. For this, we need acceptance tests, which, if explained in detail, would go beyond the scope of this chapter.

At the time of this writing, there is no acceptance testing framework that is implemented using Velocity, though there are two you can use.

Nightwatch

The `clinical:nightwatch` package allows you to run an acceptance test in a simple way as follows:

```
"Hello World" : function (client) {
    client
        .url("http://127.0.0.1:3000")
        .waitForElementVisible("body", 1000)
        .assert.title("Hello World")
        .end();
}
```

Though the installation process is not as straightforward as installing a Meteor package, you need to install and run MongoDB and PhantomJS yourself before you can run the tests.

If you want to give it a try, check out the package on atmosphere-javascript website at `https://atmospherejs.com/clinical/nightwatch`.

Laika

If you want to test the communication between the server and the client, you can use Laika. Its installation process is similar to Nightwatch, as it requires separate MongoDB and PhantomJS installations.

Laika spins up a server instance and connects multiple clients. You then can set up subscriptions or insert and modify documents. You can also test their appearance in the clients.

To install Laika, go to `http://arunoda.github.io/laika/`.

> At the time of this writing, Laika is not compatible with Velocity, which tries to run all the files in the test folder in Laika's environment, causing errors.

Summary

In this final chapter, we learned how to write simple unit tests using the `sanjo:jasmine` package for Meteor's official testing framework, Velocity. We also took a brief look at possible acceptance test frameworks.

If you want to dig deeper into testing, you can take a look at the following resources:

- `http://velocity.meteor.com`
- `http://jasmine.github.io`
- `http://www.cheatography.com/citguy/cheat-sheets/jasmine-js-testing`
- `http://doctorllama.wordpress.com/2014/09/22/bullet-proof-internationalised-meteor-applications-with-velocity-unit-testing-integration-testing-and-jasmine/`
- `http://arunoda.github.io/laika/`
- `https://github.com/xolvio/velocity`

You can find this chapter's code files at `https://www.packtpub.com/books/content/support/17713` or on GitHub at `https://github.com/frozeman/book-building-single-page-web-apps-with-meteor/tree/chapter12`.

Now that you have read the whole book, I assume you know a lot more about Meteor than before and are as excited about this framework as I am!

If you have any questions concerning Meteor, you can always ask them at `http://stackoverflow.com`, which has a great Meteor community.

I also recommend reading through all Meteor subprojects at `https://www.meteor.com/projects`, and study the documentation at `https://docs.meteor.com`.

I hope you had a great time reading this book and you're now ready to start making great apps using Meteor!

Appendix

This appendix contains a list of Meteor's command-line tool commands and a short description of `iron:router` hooks.

List of Meteor's command-line tool commands

Option	Description
`run`	Using `meteor run` is the same as using `meteor`. This will start a Meteor server for our app and watch file changes.
`create <name>`	This will initialize a Meteor project by creating a folder with the same name with some initial files.
`update`	This will update our current Meteor app to the latest release. We can also use `meteor update --release xyz` to fix our Meteor app to a specific release.
`deploy <site name>`	This will deploy our Meteor app to `<site name>.meteor.com`.

We can pass the `--delete` option to remove a deployed app |
| `build <folder_name>` | This will create a folder with our bundled app(s) code ready to be deployed on our own server. |

Option	Description
`add/remove <package name>`	This will add or remove a Meteor core package to/from our project.
`list`	This will list all Meteor packages our app is using.
`mongo`	This will give us access to our local MongoDB shell. We need to also have our application started with `meteor run` at the same time. If we need access to the mongo database of a app deployed on `meteor.com`, use `$ meteor mongo yourapp.meteor.com --url` But be aware that these credentials are only valid for 1 minute.
`reset`	This will reset our local development database to a fresh state. This won't work when our application is running. Be aware that this will remove all our data stored in our local database.
`logs <site name>`	This will download and display the logs for an app we deployed at `<site name>.meteor.com`
`search`	This searches for Meteor packages and releases, whose names contain the specified regular expression.
`show`	This shows more information about a specific package or release: name, summary, the usernames of its maintainers, and, if specified, its home page and Git URL.
`publish`	This publishes our packages. We must before go to the package folder using the cd command, log in to our Meteor account using `$ meteor login`. To publish a package for the first time, we use `$ meteor publish --create`.

Option	Description
publish-for-arch	This publishes a build of an existing package version from a different architecture. *Our machine must have the right architecture to be able to publish for a specific one.* Currently, the supported architectures for Meteor are 32-bit Linux, 64-bit Linux, and Mac OS. The servers for Meteor deploy run with a 64-bit Linux.
publish-release	This publishes a release of Meteor. This takes in a JSON configuration file. For more detail, visit https://docs.meteor.com/#/full/meteorpublishrelease.
claim	This claims a site deployed with an old Meteor version with our Meteor developer account.
login	This logs us in to our Meteor developer account.
logout	This logs us out of our Meteor developer account.
whoami	This prints the username of our Meteor developer account.
test-packages	This will run tests for one or more packages. For more information, refer to *Chapter 12, Testing with Meteor.*
admin	This catches for miscellaneous commands that require authorization to use. Some example uses of meteor admin include adding and removing package maintainers and setting a home page for a package. It also includes various help functions for managing a Meteor release.

The iron:router hooks

The following table contains a list of router controller hooks:

`action`	This function can overwrite the default behavior of the route. If we define this function, we have to manually render the template using `this.render()`.
`onBeforeAction`	This function runs before the route gets rendered. Here, we can put extra custom actions.
`onAfterAction`	This function runs after the route gets rendered. Here, we can put extra custom actions.
`onRun`	This function runs once when the route is first loaded. This function doesn't run again on a hot code reloads or when the same URL is navigated again.
`onRerun`	This function will be called every time the route is called.
`onStop`	This function runs once when leaving the current route to a new route.
`subscriptions`	This function can return subscription(s) that affect `this.ready()` in the action hooks
`waitOn`	This function can return subscription(s), but will automatically render the `loadingTemplate` until those are ready.
`data`	The return value of this function will be set as the data context of this routes template.

A full explanation of these hooks can be found at the following resources:

- `https://github.com/EventedMind/iron-router/blob/devel/Guide.md#layouts`
- `https://github.com/EventedMind/iron-router/blob/devel/Guide.md#hooks`
- `https://github.com/EventedMind/iron-router/blob/devel/Guide.md#rendering-templates-with-data`

Index

Symbols

{{#each}} block helper 34
{{#if}} block helper 38
{{/myBlockHelper}} helper 38
{{#myBlockHelper}} helper 38
{{myProperty}} helper 38
{{> myTemplate}} helper 38
{{#unless}} block helper 38
{{#with}} block helper
  about 38
  using 29

A

About route
  creating 71, 72
acceptance test
  about 156, 169
  Laika 169
  Nightwatch 169
accounts packages
  about 94
  adding 94, 95
admin functionality, adding to templates
  about 95
  link, adding for edit posts 96
  link, adding for new posts 95, 96
  login form, adding 96
admin routes
  creating 101, 102
  visitors, preventing from viewing 103
admin user
  creating 98

  permissions, adding 98, 99
  routes, creating 101, 102
  security 100
advanced reactive objects 131
advanced timer object
  creating 126-128
allow rules
  adding 110, 111
app
  creating 11
  deploying 133
  deploying, on meteor.com 134
  deploying, on other servers 138
  drop-in-place style files 13
  folder structure, creating 12
  testing 155, 160
app deployment, on meteor.com
  about 134-136
  databases, backing up 137, 138
  databases, restoring 137, 138
  domain name, used 137
app deployment, on other servers
  about 138
  app, building 138, 139
  Demeteorizer, using 140
  Meteor Up (mup), using 140-143
Atmosphere
  URL 145
autopublish package
  removing 55

B

basic templates
  building 24, 25

Thank you for buying
Building Single-page Web Apps
with Meteor

About Packt Publishing

Packt, pronounced 'packed', published its first book "*Mastering phpMyAdmin for Effective MySQL Management*" in April 2004 and subsequently continued to specialize in publishing highly focused books on specific technologies and solutions.

Our books and publications share the experiences of your fellow IT professionals in adapting and customizing today's systems, applications, and frameworks. Our solution based books give you the knowledge and power to customize the software and technologies you're using to get the job done. Packt books are more specific and less general than the IT books you have seen in the past. Our unique business model allows us to bring you more focused information, giving you more of what you need to know, and less of what you don't.

Packt is a modern, yet unique publishing company, which focuses on producing quality, cutting-edge books for communities of developers, administrators, and newbies alike. For more information, please visit our website: www.packtpub.com.

About Packt Open Source

In 2010, Packt launched two new brands, Packt Open Source and Packt Enterprise, in order to continue its focus on specialization. This book is part of the Packt Open Source brand, home to books published on software built around Open Source licenses, and offering information to anybody from advanced developers to budding web designers. The Open Source brand also runs Packt's Open Source Royalty Scheme, by which Packt gives a royalty to each Open Source project about whose software a book is sold.

Writing for Packt

We welcome all inquiries from people who are interested in authoring. Book proposals should be sent to author@packtpub.com. If your book idea is still at an early stage and you would like to discuss it first before writing a formal book proposal, contact us; one of our commissioning editors will get in touch with you.

We're not just looking for published authors; if you have strong technical skills but no writing experience, our experienced editors can help you develop a writing career, or simply get some additional reward for your expertise.

Getting Started with Meteor.js JavaScript Framework

ISBN: 978-1-78216-082-3   Paperback: 130 pages

Develop modern web applications in Meteor, one of the hottest new JavaScript platforms

1. Create dynamic, multiuser web applications completely in JavaScript.

2. Use best practice design patterns including MVC, templates, and data synchronization.

3. Create simple, effective user authentication including Facebook and Twitter integration.

4. Learn the time-saving techniques of Meteor to code powerful, lightning-fast web apps in minutes.

Instant Meteor JavaScript Framework Starter

ISBN: 978-1-78216-342-8   Paperback: 78 pages

Enjoy creating a multi-page site, using the exciting new Meteor framework!

1. Learn something new in an Instant! A short, fast, focused guide delivering immediate results.

2. Create multipage Meteor sites.

3. Learn best practices for structuring your app for maximum efficiency.

4. Use and configure a NoSQL database.

Please check **www.PacktPub.com** for information on our titles

Node Security

ISBN: 978-1-78328-149-7   Paperback: 94 pages

Take a deep dive into the world of securing your Node applications with Node Security

1. Examine security features and vulnerabilities within JavaScript.

2. Explore the Node platform, including the event loop and core modules.

3. Solve common security problems with available npm modules.

Getting Started with Backbone Marionette

ISBN: 978-1-78328-425-2   Paperback: 94 pages

Build large-scale JavaScript applications with Backbone Marionette quickly and efficiently

1. Create scalable and highly interactive web applications using one of the best frameworks for Backbone.js.

2. Learn about controllers, views, modules, events, commands, and regions.

3. Make the most out of Backbone Marionette by understanding its philosophy and applying it to real-life development tasks.

Please check **www.PacktPub.com** for information on our titles